Broad Is the Way

Wilfrid Laurier University Press
www.wlupress.wlu.ca
75 University Avenue West, Waterloo, ON, N2L 3C5
Tel: 519-884-0710 ext. 2665, Fax: 519-725-1399
Toll-free: 866-836-5551, Email: press@wlu.ca

Broad Is the Way: Stories from Mayerthorpe
Margaret Norquay

$24.95 • Paper • 120 pp. • April 2008
ISBN10: 1-55458-020-X • ISBN13: 978-1-55458-020-0
Life Writing Series

We are pleased to send you this book for review. We would appreciate receiving two copies of any review you might give it.

For more information please contact Clare Hitchens at 519-884-0710 ext. 2665, clare@press.wlu.ca

Mayerthorpe, Alberta, circa 1950

Broad Is the Way

Stories from Mayerthorpe

Margaret Norquay

Wilfrid Laurier University Press

[WLU]

We acknowledge the support of the Canada Council for the Arts for our publishing program. We acknowledge the financial support of the Government of Canada through the Book Publishing Industry Development Program for our publishing activities.

Library and Archives Canada Cataloguing in Publication

Norquay, Margaret, 1920–
    Broad is the way : stories from Mayerthorpe / Margaret Norquay.

(Life writing series)
ISBN 978-1-55458-020-0

    1. Norquay, Margaret, 1920– 2. Mayerthorpe (Alta.)—History. 3. Spouses of clergy—Alberta—Mayerthorpe—Biography. 4. Mayerthorpe (Alta.)—Biography. I. Title. II. Series.

FC3699.M39N67 2008   971.23'303092   C2007-907608-4

Cover design by Blakeley. Text design by Catharine Bonas-Taylor.

© 2008 Margaret Norquay

∞

This book is printed on Ancient Forest Friendly paper (100% post-consumer recycled).

Printed in Canada

Published by Wilfrid Laurier University Press
Waterloo, Ontario, Canada
www.wlupress.wlu.ca

Contents

Foreword by Sara Norquay   vii

Preface   ix

1   As the Twig Is Bent   1

2   Holy Matrimony   8

3   We Arrive in Mayerthorpe   14

4   Not by Bread Alone   21

5   Money Back Guaranteed   25

6   No Hornets Here   28

7   Mr. Kringsberg's Christmas Dinner   31

8   In a Pinch, Use Tarpaper   35

9   Sweet Singing in the Choir   40

10   Nobody Asked Me to Buy a Ticket   44

11   No 911 in the 1950s   47

12   Don't Tell Your Husband Everything   51

13   Best to Hang On to a Big Jack   54

14   Glad We Didn't Have Noah's Animals   56

15   Never Mess with the WCTU   61

16   You Need to Dress Up for a Wedding   64

17   Purged of Pity and Fear   69

18   Too Bad They Don't Brew Beer   73

19   Scrub Trees May Have Deep Roots   78

20   Sympathy and Prejudice Come with a Crack on the Head   83

21   Recycling Gallon Cans   87

22   Founding Edmonton's United Community Fund   92

23   Learning to Be a Woman   98

Foreword

My mother, Marg Norquay, has always been a storyteller. When I was young, she often said that one day she would write a book. Sometime after she retired for the second or third time, I started asking her to write her stories down. Finally, she took a writing class with Beth Kaplan, and soon the stories poured forth. This book is a selection of what she wrote over the last seven or eight years.

These stories were originally written as individual pieces, so the chapters read as if they were being remembered; the telling of one story reminds the storyteller of the next without strict concern for chronology.

The stories reveal my mother's slow awakening to an understanding that other people often had expectations of her that she didn't recognize or didn't meet. The first story of her upbringing helps explain her later reactions to living as a minister's wife in Mayerthorpe from 1949 to 1955, when most of the stories take place.

My father, Jim, was born in 1919 and grew up in the town of Conniston, near Sudbury, in Northern Ontario. He went to Victoria College at the University of Toronto, where he met my mother. He did his fieldwork as a young divinity student in the Peace River country of Northern Alberta. His love of the people there led him to return to Mayerthorpe, when he accepted his first pastoral charge. In the 1970s, when I travelled there with him to visit his old parishes, we met many people who remembered him and welcomed us into their homes to reminisce.

My mother was born in 1920 and grew up on an acreage near Port Credit, Ontario, which is now part of Mississauga, a suburban city west of Toronto. She served in the army during the Second World War and was the community recreation director for the town of Dunnville, Ontario, before she married Jim. She wrote her MA thesis about her experience in Dunnville.

Foreword

My parents lived in Mayerthorpe until shortly after my brother was born in 1955. Then they moved to Edmonton. My parents continued to build and run Surprise Lake Camp while they lived in Alberta.

The bear story is one of my favourites, because I remember when it happened. I was old enough to be a camper in the cabin where the tadpoles were kept in the biffy cans, but I slept through it all and was told the story. Many years later, I took my children to see Surprise Lake Camp. It still offers camping experiences to children and young people, and Uncle Bill's cabin, where our family stayed, is still there.

The Mayerthorpe stories are told as my mother remembers them, and some details, such as the cost of things, have faded from memory with the passing of years. Did the choir gowns cost exactly $350? Did they really charge fifty cents to see the amateur show? When you read about how they got rid of Huh! for $150, you need to know that the car wasn't sold until after my grandparents had given them a new Austin, a fact that is mentioned in a later story.

If you are not from the area where the stories take place, you might like to know that gumbo is the legendary sticky mud that ungravelled roads turn into after a rainstorm. It has been known to swallow cows and cars, and is one of those elements of northern life, like giant mosquitoes and flesh-eating blackflies, that live on in tall tales and family histories.

In 1962, my parents left Edmonton and moved to Toronto. There they lived and worked in church communities in a large urban setting with much the same concern for people they had in Mayerthorpe. But those stories will have to wait for a book of their own.

Sara Norquay
February 2008

Preface

The title for this collection of stories comes from Matthew 7:13 (King James Version): "... broad is the way that leadeth to destruction."

The stories were originally written for my children. The events described occurred before they were born, or when they were very young. Now, ministers' wives have their own careers—something unthinkable in the early fifties. The stories portray a time that is no more. However, readers may find some familiar truths.

When I was a young girl, dinnertime at home was spent vigorously discussing politics and economics. Sewing and baking were not emphasized. As a minister's wife, my contributions to the Ladies' Aid bake sales that supported the upkeep of the manse were limited to pouring tea. I did want to be involved in my husband's ministry. I offered to spice up the Aid meetings by arranging for guest speakers who would address the concerns of the wider church and community that I thought, as Christians, we should at least try to alleviate. But this offer was never taken up. I apparently did not fit the mould of a minister's wife and was often criticized.

However, despite the disapproval expressed by some, there were those who cheered me on. To be sure, they were a minority. But without them there might have been no stories. So my thanks go to all who helped me on the way to destruction.

Acknowledgements

The author wishes to thank the many friends, family members, and participants in the events described, without whom there would have been no stories to write. I would especially like to thank the members of Beth Kaplan's writers' group, who served as helpful critics over several years. I am also indebted to Ellen Garfield, who assisted in the preparation of the manuscript. Lastly, a thank-you to my daughter, Sara Norquay, who assisted in the editing.

one

As the Twig Is Bent

I was brought up to believe that there was nothing in the world I couldn't do, provided I was willing to work for it. It was a rather useful belief for a child to have, but as I grew up I began to realize it wasn't entirely true: I knew there were some things I'd never get to do because I was a woman. But at the time I didn't want to do any of them, so this knowledge didn't trouble me.

My mother had more education than most middle-class women of her generation, and more than anyone else in her immediate family. She graduated from Toronto General Hospital as a nurse in 1915, and this training imbued her whole life. She had also taken a six-month course in nutrition at the Toronto Technical School and, thus armed, she felt entirely competent to bring up a healthy family. In 1916 she married my father, a struggling young lawyer, and my oldest sister, the first of five children, was born one year later. We were all what were then dubbed Dr. Brown's babies, meaning that Mother followed implicitly the instructions of the current leading Toronto pediatrician. He advised my mother that I was a delicate child who "already knew too much" and that I should forego kindergarten and not attend school until my seventh birthday.

With a birthday in April, I was seven and a half by the time I entered "junior first," now called grade one. By that time, thanks to tutoring by my older sister, I had memorized word for word all of the first primer: *The little red hen she found some wheat. She called the cat. She called the dog. She called the pig. "Who will help me plant my wheat?" "Not I," said the cat—"Not I," said the dog—"Not I," said the pig.* When I got to school, I was elated when I seemed to be ahead of the whole class in reading. However, I didn't know which group of letters referred to which words, a situation my shocked teacher finally discovered. One day, with my eyes firmly fixed on the page, I "read" the wrong story. I did manage to pass at the end of the year, but I was the only one in the class whose handwriting was never judged good enough to earn a notebook, a problem that put me in constant conflict with my teacher, Miss Merton. I was sure I'd inherited my handwriting from my father, whose writing was notoriously bad. To prove the point, I insisted that when a note had to be written to my teacher explaining the reason for an absence, my father would write it for me. But Miss Merton didn't think writing was hereditary. The idea that I was delicate followed me till the end of high school. It may have been fuelled by the sorrow of my mother over the death of our baby brother who died of spinal meningitis, a death my mother mourned for many years. But as a child, I always thought it was because I looked like Aunty Gladys, my father's much-loved sister, said to have died of a heart attack. However, I was sure she died of a broken heart, because she wanted to marry a Roman Catholic and the family wouldn't let her. I never believed I was delicate, but the myth robbed me of two more years of school, one after a bout of strep throat, when I should have been in grade two, and another in high school when I had scarlet fever. The result was that when I went back to school, I worked doubly hard, determined to make up the lost time.

At the end of my first year at school, we moved to the country because my father thought that was the best place to bring up a family. He built a house on a ten-acre lot, a quarter of a mile east of Highway 10, on the old Middle Road, which later became the Queen Elizabeth Way. We moved there just after the 1929 stock market crash, which began the Depression of the thirties.

Two years previously, Dad had left a prestigious Toronto law firm, because he couldn't cope with their ethics. He was now struggling to establish a practice with his younger brother, home from the war. He couldn't tell anyone why he'd left the firm, and some may have thought he was let go. In any case, it was a difficult time to start a new law practice. Many of Dad's clients were people facing bankruptcy and unable to pay him. As recompense, Dad would get several pairs of hand-knit socks at Christmas from women we called his "little widows" or a bottle of homemade wine from our Italian neighbours— wine, which, because of Dad's strong Methodist upbringing, he never drank. Mother, swearing us girls to secrecy, gleefully put it in her Christmas cake, which she then served to the church Board when they met at our house. It was a family joke that they always asked for second helpings.

Soon after arriving at the new house, Dad began to plant a large vegetable garden and gradually added an orchard where we grew a wide variety of fruit. My brother and I dug a kind of cave in the hill at the back of the house, which Dad turned into a root cellar to store vegetables and Northern Spy apples. Eventually, we had several acres of asparagus, which we sold to the Co-op. Mother made untold jars of jam, quarts of fruit, and, according to family lore, one year canned ninety quarts of tomatoes. We also raised chickens, ducks, and turkeys, so we always had lots of eggs and a bird to cook for Sunday dinner. Money was tight all through my childhood, so raising our own food was a necessity.

In addition to the washing, ironing, and cooking needed to support four children, a husband, and my maternal grandmother, who lived with us, Mother also made all our clothes, often out of hand-me-downs. I especially remember her making me a matching jacket and skirt out of an old suit of my Dad's that she took apart. I thought it was "real sharp." By the time my sister and I were eleven and thirteen, our older relatives needed more care, so Mother, the only nurse in the family, would be called on to go off for a week or two to bring them back to health. My sister and I would be put in charge of making the meals and doing the housekeeping. Grandma was there, in case some arbiter was needed, but we learned all the basic skills of cooking, cleaning, grocery shopping, and making our own clothes. However, Grandma always insisted on helping us do the evening dinner dishes, and would entertain us with stories of her youth.

Mother had a wonderful sense of humour, which provided a good balance to my father, who sometimes didn't seem to have one; at least he never laughed at himself or made funny jokes. Mother said it was because he'd had such a struggle after his own father died, supporting his mother and his younger brother and sister. His widowed mother had been left with no income and thousands of dollars of debt. My grandfather had been a scholar with a double MA in mathematics and classics from Cambridge. Shortly after he completed his graduate degree, he'd immigrated to Canada. After a couple of years of teaching in a private boys' school, he earned a precarious living publishing and editing small-town newspapers. Dad told us that one year they had several meals of only bread and chili sauce, made by his mother. For many years, Grandfather was a stump thumper for the Liberal Party. With this credential, he wound up as deputy minister of Public Works in Ottawa. For the first time, he had some disposable income. He was a book collector, and racked up $10,000 in debt from buying rare first editions. After his death, my grandmother, not knowing the value of the books, sold them to a junk dealer for $25.

Dad was in the middle of law school when his father died, and would have dropped out had not our Auntie Charlotte, a maternal aunt who had "married well," insisted on supporting him. He supplemented his income by writing a weekly column under a pseudonym for the *Toronto Star*. In addition to supporting his mother and planning to get married, he felt duty bound to pay off all his father's debts when he graduated. In order to explain my father's serious approach to almost everything, Mother let us know this when we were all quite young.

Dad was a lifelong Mason, a lifelong Liberal, and a stump thumper as his father had been. The year Mitchell Hepburn became premier of Ontario, Dad was influential in getting our Liberal candidate, Duncan Marshall, elected. Never before in living memory had a Liberal been elected in Peel County. Because of Dad's political involvement, his work as a Mason, and his membership in the Saturday Night Club, a debating society he'd belonged to since his youth, he was always making speeches. He prided himself on making good speeches, and would prepare by carefully writing them out and then practising out loud in the furnace room, where he wouldn't be disturbed.

He also had a strong commitment to what he perceived to be the social good. He thought his children should be brought up going to church and Sunday school. When he discovered that the Cooksville Church had only an evening service, he thought there should be one in the morning so children could attend. He'd had some musical training in his youth, and told the Board that if they'd agree to have a service in the morning, he'd organize a children's choir and pay a student minister to take the service. The Board agreed, and so the choir was organized. Because of the lack of other kinds of cultural opportunities in the village, the choir was open to any child who would come to practise, regardless of whether their parents belonged to the church or not. One of the choir members was a Jewish boy with a lovely clear soprano voice. He attended regular practice and sang with us every Sunday, except for once a month, when he went to Toronto for the weekend to go to synagogue with his grandparents. All through our growing-up years, Dad conducted both the junior choir for the morning service and the senior choir, which sang in the evening. By the time we got to high school, we children were singing in both choirs.

Dad was demanding as a parent, and though we adored him, we were also a bit afraid of him. He could get very angry at any misbehaviour, but never laid a hand on us and never said a word to belittle us. It was important to him that we all did well in school, but he seemed able to moderate his demands in relation to what he perceived to be our particular capabilities.

Knowing Dad thought speech-making an important skill, I always entered the high school's annual oratorical contest and practised in the furnace room. Because of the specific demands he made on me, I've wondered in retrospect if he wasn't disappointed that I hadn't been a boy, since his first child was a girl. He struck a bargain with me that he'd give me a dollar if I stood first in my class in high school, provided that after having once done so, I'd give him back fifty cents any time I didn't. I *didn't* always stand first, but it was a bargain he never collected on, and probably never intended to.

He thought it was most important that all his children were able to think, so dinner always took at least an hour. Dad would start a family discussion, baiting us with some outrageous remark that would get us all arguing with each other. A full set of the *Encyclopedia Britannica* was housed in our dining room. If the argument was about some fact, we'd eventually resolve it by looking it up, but never until we'd exhausted all our collective knowledge and ignorance. If the argument was about an idea, we might still use the encyclopedia to get additional information, but it could rarely be used to settle the matter. Our grandmother was a dyed-in-the-wool Conservative, so often the talk would turn to politics. Once we were all furiously arguing with one another, Dad would finally have had enough and would leave the table; we knew we'd swallowed his bait once again. He continued this practice until we all left home. During my university days, it was one of the attractions our home had for fellow students, whom we'd bring along for a home-cooked meal. I remember an uproarious discussion we had when Dad said a lot of social workers were just Nosey Parkers and the Children's Aid should not be the sole arbiter in child adoptions.

Mother seldom took part in these discussions, apparently happy to let Dad take over this aspect of our upbringing. However, she took a sustained interest in everything we did or wanted to do. For example, I still couldn't sing in tune at the age of eight, although everyone else in the family could. Because Dad thought all his children should be able to sing in tune almost as soon as they could talk, I badly wanted to sing like my brother and sisters. So Mother worked with me at the piano until I could and then, to prove it, made me perform for the whole family. I still remember the song, from the book called *Highroads of Song: Oh how I do love to go up in a swing / Up in the air so high*. When we got involved in school activities and needed a prop or a costume for the high school play, Mother would help us find it or make it. She put up with my brother practising his trombone in the kitchen when she was cooking dinner, and my sister practising for a music exam and banging on the piano when she couldn't get something quite right. If I got stuck on a play I was writing or a speech I was planning to make at the student assembly, she'd critique it or ask me questions until I figured out where to go next. Sometimes, when I had no particular project in mind, I'd get an idea from some casual remark she made. The plot line for *Corner Cupboards for Cora*,* the play that won an award at the Peel Music Festival, stemmed from Mother telling us she hated the china cabinet she'd inherited from her mother, and wished she could afford to replace it with corner cupboards. The play, at least, solved the problem.

Despite looking after a family of seven, Mother still had time for good works in the community. We lived close enough to the Middle Road School to get home for lunch, but Mother worried about the farm children who lived too far away to walk home—especially in winter. She organized the first Home and School in the district to raise money to employ someone to make hot cocoa every noon hour. When she discovered a nearby Chinese family who had a boy with cerebral palsy who couldn't be accommodated at the local school, she tried to get the Imperial Order of the Daughters of the Empire to raise money for transportation to take him to the school for disabled children in Toronto. When the IODE turned her down, because he wasn't "a Canadian," she was incensed, but she persuaded the Lions Club to take him on. For several years she picked and sold our apples so she

---

* In the play, Cora gets her corner cupboards by going into debt. The bailiff turns up at her house saying he'll have to take some furniture in payment. She begs him to take anything but her china cabinet, which she claims is very valuable. Of course, the bailiff takes it, saying it will just nicely cover her debt.

could raise money for the Chinese family to buy books and school supplies. She was delighted when he not only finished high school but graduated from university.

We took for granted so much of what Mother did. When we were living in residence at university, money was so uncertain that we never knew from one term to the next whether we'd be able to continue. I had to spend another year in high school after I'd passed all my fifth-form (grade thirteen) exams because there was no money to finance my first year. We earned some money every spring from the asparagus and from picking strawberries in the summer, but there were no McDonald's or Starbucks to employ students. When our oldest great-aunt died, a schoolteacher who Mother had nursed, she left Mother $15,000. Mother didn't spend a cent of it on herself but on helping to get three of us through university. For six or seven years Mother never had any new clothes, but we didn't notice. We just thought she did what mothers do.

two

Holy Matrimony

Years passed, and now, as a young married woman, I became aware that my suitability as the minister's wife was in some question. I had not only been overdressed at my first appearance but had taken down the green plastic curtains on our bedroom windows, which horrified the secretary of the Ladies' Aid, who noticed the bare windows on her way to the post office and spread the news. There was no one across the road from us to see in, except for a few cows. But, as she pointedly told everyone, the Catholic priest lived on the other side of the road only a block down.

Having apparently scandalized the Ladies' Aid, I found myself wondering what people thought about Jim's car when he drove into town from Peace River to become their new minister. Buying a car was an almost insurmountable obstacle for most young ministers starting out on their first charge, and Jim's car was unlike any that had been seen in Mayerthorpe for twelve or fifteen years. Jim's father had offered to buy a car for him when he went on his mission field to Peace River. It was nearing the end of the war, when new cars were difficult to get and only a few good second-hand ones were available. His father said he'd pay for whatever Jim wanted, but Jim, not wishing to spend too much of his father's money, got the cheapest one he could find—a 1928 Model A Victoria Coupe, for which he paid $500. It was a two-seater, high off the ground, with a rumble seat at the back. When his father saw it, he was obviously disappointed that Jim hadn't got a more recent model, but all he said was "Huh!" So from then on Jim called the car Huh! By the time I arrived, however, whatever may have been said or thought about Huh! had probably run its course.

The editor and sole reporter of the *Mayerthorpe Review* felt he would be expected to write something about the minister's wedding. Without consulting us, he wrote a note about it in what was popularly

Jim and Huh!

called his "Hatches, Matches and Dispatches" column. He said the minister and his wife had enjoyed a couple of weeks in Niagara Falls for their honeymoon. I hoped no one would ask me any details about the Falls. Not being a good liar, I'd have felt obliged to say that we hadn't gone to the Falls, but had gone camping in Algonquin Park— a honeymoon destination probably inexplicable to people whose parents still had memories of the hardships of living in tents while they wrestled their farms out of virgin forest.

A few days after we arrived in Mayerthorpe, I was sitting out on the front porch in the middle of the morning, reading a thick book related to my thesis, when a parishioner came by and said, "Here's the new bride, looking up a recipe." I quickly put my hand over the title, closed the book and said, "Oh, I was just doing a little reading," knowing that was not what any self-respecting housewife should be doing at that hour of the morning. I couldn't tell her I was looking up references for my thesis, which I had been working on when Jim and I decided to get married.

At the time we made the decision, Jim was serving his first year as minister in Mayerthorpe, and I was in Toronto, halfway through my MA in sociology at the University of Toronto. Jim had not figured in my plans when I began the program, and I was determined to finish it. We had gone to university together, but neither of us had seen the other as a possible marriage partner or even as a date. We had often gone to dances in the same group of friends, but we'd always been with someone else. We'd worked on some of the same committees, and in my last year we jointly ran a major student organization. We'd had fun working together and had initiated several new programs, including the establishment of the first International Students' Organization, a group that aimed to support students from other countries. After graduation we went our separate ways. Jim had a pastoral charge in the Peace River Country, and I did a stint in the Canadian Women's Army Corps. We didn't see each other for almost four years, though we kept in touch with the odd Christmas card. It wasn't until I became the community recreational director of the town of Dunnville, Ontario, and Jim was back in Toronto doing his MA in philosophy that we got together again.

Even then we mightn't have seen much of each other, had the Recreational Council not been going through great turmoil over funding and an ongoing fight with the town council. Over a nine-month period, I resigned, was rehired, and let go twice. When not on the job, I'd be home in Cooksville, Jim and I would see each other, and he'd get the details of what was happening. When I'd go back to Dunnville, he'd come to see me there, joking that he couldn't wait to find out what cliff I was then hanging from. I found, to my surprise, that we had interests in common that we'd never discovered before, and gradually we began falling in love.

I finally quit the Dunnville job a few weeks before Jim finished his studies and left for Mayerthorpe. By that time we were seriously talking about marriage, but neither of us was sure enough to get engaged formally. Jim was looking forward to his new charge, and I was intent on writing my thesis about the Dunnville experience and finishing my MA. However, just before I left Dunnville, Jim covered his bases by phoning my father at his office and inviting him to lunch. Jim told me afterwards he'd just thought it a good idea to get to know him a bit. I'm sure he didn't tell him he wanted to marry his daughter, because we were still very tentative, and he would have known that I thought asking my father's permission was ridiculous.

The next year we corresponded with some regularity, and Jim came back to Toronto for Christmas, which he spent with my family. By this time, despite some ups and downs, and struggling, among other

Jim and Marg getting engaged under the quilt, Christmas 1948

things, to figure out a yearly budget on a minister's annual salary of
$1,800, we had decided to get engaged. We hadn't yet broken the news
to anybody, though I'm sure my family was wondering what was going
on between us. On Christmas Day, when we had finished giving out
all the presents, my mother picked up a large suit box still under the
tree and gave it to us. *To Marg and Jim from the Cooksville Ladies'
Aid*, it said. Jim and I were sitting beside each other on Grandma's big
chesterfield, and Jim opened the box with glee. He pulled out a large
double handmade patchwork quilt, threw it over the two of us and
said, "Would you share this with me in Northern Alberta?" So our
engagement was announced. Mother, betting that we were going to tie
the knot, had commissioned the Ladies' Aid to make the quilt. On
second thought, maybe Jim did tell my Dad that we were thinking of
getting married, and Dad told Mother. After Christmas, Jim went back
to Mayerthorpe and I worked on my thesis, hoping to have the first
draft done by summer.

The wedding was originally planned for July. But Jim wrote to say
he was planning to take some of the young village boys on a camping
trip scheduled for a few days after our arrival in Mayerthorpe. "Nuts
to that," I said. "I'm darned if I'm going to be left alone in a strange
place right after our marriage." So we postponed the wedding until the
end of August, a few weeks after the camping trip. I was relieved,

because my thesis wasn't going as well as I had hoped, and I needed another month on it. However, when June came, I thought I'd better begin to think about the wedding.

I wanted to have it outside in the sunken garden—a nice, flat piece of lawn down the hill behind our house, beside the pond. I wanted to have a square dance on the green afterwards and serve box lunches to the guests. But my mother wouldn't hear of it. My older sister had been married in the local church, and my parents had catered an elaborate dinner at a restaurant for extended family and friends. Mother wanted to do the same for me. Unlike my sister, who got a big bang out of planning her wedding, I regarded it as a nuisance, something I had to do but wanted to be done with. If we couldn't have the kind of party I wanted, I really didn't care what we did. But it wasn't worth having a scrap; I was too busy getting my thesis written. So I told my mother to plan the wedding any way she liked and I would try to come.

Then there was the question of the trousseau. My aunt told me she'd like to do something for my wedding. Would I like a trousseau tea or a family dinner party? I didn't want a trousseau tea, where the guests would be given a showing of all the things the bride had put together to help her begin her new life: towels, table and bed linens, lingerie, even the wedding nightgown. I opted for the family dinner party. And there was the matter of what I would wear for the wedding. I didn't want a white dress and a bridal veil. I thought I should have something I might possibly wear again. So Mother and I went shopping. We bought a pattern I could live with and some ice-blue lace material that Mother made into a lovely dress. We got a milliner to make a large brimmed hat out of the lace. We dyed white linen pumps to match the dress, and the wedding costume was complete.

Newspapers in the 1940s were full of details about weddings, including descriptions of the bride's and the bridesmaids' dresses and the bride's going-away costume. She was expected to change into this, throw her bouquet to the guests, say goodbye, and only then leave for the honeymoon. I had an elegant suit with a coat to match, made by my father's tailor. But we had a different plan. Jim and I were going camping in Algonquin Park. I had no intention of going away in a suit and high heels and having to change at the first service station en route. We decided on camp clothes in contrasting colours. I made a red flannel shirt to wear with royal-blue wool slacks; Jim's shirt was bright yellow, worn with grey slacks. We were all set to paddle from the landing across the lake to the family cabin. When my very proper aunt asked me what I was going to wear for going away, I said I'd had a new tailored suit made. I didn't add that I wasn't going to wear it.

Next, there was the matter of figuring out how to get back to Mayerthorpe from Toronto. Jim said that Charlie Bromley, who helped out with funerals in Mayerthorpe, needed a new panel truck, and that it would cost him much less if he could find someone to drive it from Toronto. Jim said we might offer to do it for him and save on train fare. I thought it would be great fun to say we were driving to our new home in a hearse. However, Charlie changed his mind and decided to wait another year before making the purchase, so that was that. It would have made a great story to tell my grandchildren.

We didn't arrange to have any official photographs taken because Uncle Eddie, my father's brother, offered to take candid shots throughout the whole proceedings. His photos before the wedding are most informative. Jim's show a man obviously very uncomfortable, if not terrified, whereas I look confident and happy. However, during the ceremony Jim was able to repeat the vows in a loud, clear voice, whereas I was so overcome with emotion that I couldn't repeat any of them for fear of bursting into tears. My friends all said it was the first time they had ever seen me speechless. Jim was clearly married to me, but they weren't sure I was married to him.

After the dinner, we were finally able to say goodbye to our guests, go home, and change into our going-away clothes. We had borrowed an ancient car from Jim's brother Eddie, which he'd brought down from Sudbury. Our two families gathered to see us off. As we left the driveway, we could tell by the sound that Eddie must have tied a bunch of tin cans to the bumper. We didn't look until we stopped for gas at the first garage out of the city. Jim got out to check the tires and pay the attendant, and I looked at him and thought, "Gosh, what have I done? Do I really know this man?"

When Jim got back in the car he was chuckling. "I cut the rope holding the cans together," he said, "but Eddie put a big sign on the back of the trunk that says, in large letters, AMATEUR NIGHT TONIGHT."

three

We Arrive in Mayerthorpe

I should have known what I was getting into when I got married in August 1949, for I couldn't claim the innocence of most unsuspecting young girls who marry ministers. I knew quite well what it was to live in a community to which one could never belong. When I was a small child, my family had moved from Toronto to the countryside, to live on farmland between two small villages. My father commuted to the city to his law practice—something none of my classmates' fathers did. We went to school in Port Credit, Ontario, and to church in nearby Cooksville. I learned at an early age that the only way one can really belong to a small community is to be born there.

And long before I had any idea I might end up marrying a parson, I had a clear picture of the odd sort of people some communities expect their minister and wife and family to be. When I was growing up, the minister's children very often spent Sunday afternoons at our place. Since we lived two miles out of the village and had no close neighbours, they were free to enjoy youthful hijinks without anyone being the wiser.

These pastimes were harmless: skating on the pond in winter, swimming in it in summer, singing and playing instruments around our piano, and for a short interval walking around on homemade stilts. We once organized a circus. The wife of one of our ministers told my mother that she dare not let her son even play catch in their backyard on Sunday afternoon because the neighbours would object. I knew at an early age that such a circumscribed life was not for me.

When I finally took the plunge and got engaged to Jim, no one was more surprised than I. I had no doubts about the man—that was what did me in—but I was really concerned about the profession, or perhaps I should say the institution, into which I was marrying. Some of my friends, who ought to have known better, acted as if they expected me to change my personality overnight. They began to edit their speech when I was with them. They would start to tell a good story and then stop and apologize for telling it to me. The alarming thing was that they were not trying to be funny. They were supposedly being considerate, though of what I was not sure.

In addition, I was given all kinds of advice from ministers and their wives who were friends of my family, some conflicting, some helpful, and some I was never able to test. (One gave me a book written by a minister's daughter, which turned out to be a eulogy of her sainted mother. When I read it, I felt anything but saintly.) When I learned that our first home would be in a small village of four hundred people in northern Alberta, I was relieved. All the Westerners I had ever met had been warm and friendly people. They surely wouldn't have the rigid expectations concerning their minister's wife that had been current in my childhood. If I was going to marry a parson, I was certain that it would be easier for me to settle in the West than in the more formal East, and I was happy about the prospect.

An elderly and very wise minister admonished me never to make any remarks about my husband's sermon on a Sunday. Comment, if any, should be reserved until at least Wednesday. By that time I would have forgotten the point I wanted to make and that would be just as well. This was the most valuable suggestion of any I was given, but I found it difficult if not impossible to follow.

I wrote Jim, then in Mayerthorpe, that all this advice was giving me terribly cold feet about our forthcoming marriage. He didn't seem to take me seriously, and we never discussed it further. But at the family dinner held before the wedding, he made a short speech and then with considerable flourish presented me with a pair of bed socks.

Jim began sending me pictures of the manse, inside and out, so that we could plan what we needed to take. I thought the house a little small, but at least it was a house. Many of my married friends, caught by the postwar housing shortage, were forced to live in rented rooms. Those who were most stunned to learn I was marrying a minister said, "Well, at least you found a man with a house."

I was concerned when I realized that the plumbing facilities consisted of a rain barrel and a footpath to an outhouse. Jim explained the plumbing by saying that of course we had running water, only we had to run after it. So I began accumulating an assortment of enamel-ware, including a large basin for taking a Saturday-night bath and a diaper pail, which I thought would be easier to sit on than a chamber pot. The village was served by two community wells. No homeowner had his own well because the water level was so low and the cost of drilling prohibitive. Most people had their water delivered by a horse-drawn wagon; the water was free, but delivery cost fifty cents a barrel. Jim had collected some old oil drums, which fitted nicely on the bumper of his Model A Ford, and he found that four of them would do a washing in the old wringer washer that stood in the back kitchen.

I looked up Mayerthorpe on the map and discovered it at the extreme edge of a line of obscure dots. If not actually in the wilderness, it was certainly on the edge of it. My father, who had never been west of Port Arthur, Ontario, declared that he couldn't see why anyone, much less his daughter, would want to go to such God-forsaken country. He didn't even smile when I teased him that it couldn't be God-forsaken if Jim was there. When I realized the tiny village of Mayerthorpe was the largest community along a line 115 miles long, and remembered that our Model A Ford could only go thirty jerky miles an hour, I decided to prepare for a long cultural drought.

Whereas most girls buy a trousseau of lace, frills, and table linen, I bought records and books and some favourite prints from the Art Gallery of Toronto (now the Art Gallery of Ontario). Since my mother had brought me up to believe in the importance of hyacinths to feed the soul, such things seemed necessities. If I was going to a cultural desert, I would take along the tools to build an oasis. My one extravagance was twenty dollars for some embroidered Chinese silk to make a jacket for a pair of lounging pyjamas. The town looked a little grey and dreary in the photographs Jim had sent, and I thought I might need some colour. Little did I realize that I would seldom have time to lounge, and if I did, I would be sure to be caught by some shocked parishioner coming to the door to see my husband.

In late September, we arrived in Edmonton by train, at the unearthly hour of 6 a.m. A friend, in whose yard our Model A had been parked during the month Jim had been off getting married, met us. We had our breakfast, climbed into the old car, and began the ninety-mile trip.

I was astonished to discover that the road to Mayerthorpe, which Jim had blithely called a highway, was not paved, scarcely gravelled, and had only one lane. "Lane" just about described it. I was to learn that the word "highway" was a euphemism for the only road leading to the largest town on its route. It had nothing to do either with its condition or construction. However, the sun was shining, the leaves were a beautiful golden yellow, and we were going to our new home. I was unprepared for the endless miles of bush that hugged the road, unlike any farming country I had ever seen. Jim told me it was one of the last frontiers. In 1949, people in that area were still settling on farmland that had yet to be broken for the first time.

As the afternoon wore on, it got warm. The car's manifold, which produced heat only in warm weather, never in winter, made my feet so hot I had to hang them out the window, there being no room in the car to put them anywhere else. I should have cherished that heat because it was the last time I was warm for months.

About suppertime, when Jim said we had only a couple of miles to go, we began to see a few straggling frame houses and then two grain elevators etched against the sky. Suddenly, a sign appeared: Mayerthorpe population 420. We turned onto the main street. I remember a clutter of buildings: a hardware store, a bank, a Co-op, a gas station, a John Deere farm implements dealer, a pool hall and a small post office. Jim turned a corner and said, "We're here!"

And there stood two small wood-frame buildings side by side, both in need of paint. The first building had a peaked roof and looked to be one room with a basement. The sign in front said Mayerthorpe United Church. The other building, which I took to be the manse, was two storeys, with steps leading up to an open porch.

I bounded from the car, anxious to see inside. Jim brought in our bags and then went for kindling to light the stove. I ran to the living room to see if the wallpaper was as bad as it had looked in the snapshot. Fortunately, it wasn't—quite. Our pictures might look all right, after all. I was trying to decide where to hang them when Jim asked if I wasn't interested in the kitchen. When I said I wasn't specially, he sounded disappointed, so I went out. Jim had lit a fire in the stove and had bacon and eggs in the pan. And then I saw it—a tap! A sink and tap! I wondered where they could have come from. Jim twinkled, and I remembered he had talked in recent letters about a surprise he was working on.

He had rigged up a gravity water system. True, the water still had to be hauled in barrels from the town well, but he had put a fifty-gallon galvanized tank in the cellar and another one upstairs on the second floor. These were joined by water pipes he had threaded and

Mayerthorpe United Church in the mid-1950s

fitted by himself. He had knocked a hole in the outside wall of the house through which he could empty the barrels of water into the cellar tank. A hand pump, attached to the pipes, pumped the water up two storeys to the upper tank. When I wanted water in the kitchen, I could just turn on the tap and the water would flow down. Remarkable! It was the talk of the town. True, the drainage system consisted of a single pail in the cupboard under the sink, but the system had every appearance of convenience and I was delighted. I didn't foresee the day when I would leave the tap on and be called from the back kitchen by excited children telling me that water was pouring out the front door and onto the sidewalk.

A snapshot of the manse living room that Jim sent to Marg in the spring of 1949

Jim's first service was two days later on Sunday evening, and he said he expected a full house. I was terrified. I would have given anything to stay away, but I knew that to do so would be thought scandalous and would make a very bad beginning. So we arrived at the door of the church on the dot of 7:30 and, true enough, the place was packed. I was wearing a new suit and matching coat with a fashionable hemline several inches below my knees. It was considered the latest style in Toronto. In a flash, I realized that the low hemline had not yet reached Mayerthorpe, and I felt terribly and conspicuously overdressed; for sure they would take me for a stuck-up Easterner. The door creaked as we walked in, and the entire congregation turned to look at the minister's new wife. I slunk into the nearest empty seat as fast as I could, and Jim began the service.

Afterwards, I was ashamed of my fears because everyone was so friendly. As I expected, the first question was "How do you like the West?"

I said I hadn't been there long enough to know, but I had come expecting to like it, and was sure I would.

A gruff old man said, "It's all right if you don't stay too long." I asked him how long he had been here. "All my life," he replied. "I was born here."

I realized soon after that the question about whether I would like the West was no idle one. Jim and I were on some kind of trial. The only other young ministers in Mayerthorpe's experience had stayed but a few months. Both left after their marriage to Eastern girls. I was not expected either to like the West or want my husband to stay in it. Well, I thought, we'll show them. And we did. But that beautiful lounging jacket never left my closet.

four

Not by Bread Alone

Within weeks after Jim and I arrived in Mayerthorpe, I invited the Ladies' Aid to meet in the parsonage. When it was time for refreshments, the woman who had offered to help serve the lunch asked whether I had made the coffee. I said that I had made tea, assuming it wouldn't matter. But I could tell by the woman's face that I'd given the wrong answer. Afterwards, I kicked myself that I hadn't caught on that coffee was the drink of choice in the community—at least among the women. I hadn't taken in the significance of a percolating coffee pot on the back of the stove in every home in which I'd been since our arrival. I'd simply followed the practice in my parent's home of serving tea in the evening—never coffee—lest you might not sleep well.

While we were eating lunch, one woman commented that she'd never seen such large pictures in anyone's parlour. She was particularly struck with Tom Thomson's *Spring Ice*. "What a beautiful oil painting. Did you paint it, Mrs. Norquay?" Trying not to embarrass her, I fumbled to explain that it was only a print, a copy of a painting by an artist of whom I was particularly fond.

An older woman who had lived in Edmonton for some years after a career teaching in one-room rural schools asked if she could look at our books, which we'd shelved in stacked orange crates. She said she loved books, but with neither a library nor a bookstore in town, she hadn't had anything to read since she'd come to Mayerthorpe to be near to her married son. She couldn't get much out of reading Eaton's catalogue. Then seeing, a copy of Spengler's *Decline of the West* sitting on top of our improvised bookcase, she read out in a puzzled, almost angry voice, "*Decline of the West*—what's that about? Why do Easterners think we're declining?" I struggled to explain that Spengler wasn't talking about the western provinces but about the decline of Western civilization. Her look indicated this answer hadn't helped.

The president quickly intervened, saying we needed to decide where the aid would go for their next meeting, thus saving me from having to explain what Western civilization meant. But I knew I had touched a sore spot and hoped I hadn't made it worse.

I was beginning to realize that I had a lot to learn about getting along in the community, about bridging the gap between myself, with an essentially urban background from southern Ontario, and the people we would be working with. I wondered if I'd inadvertently created more questions about my suitability as the parson's wife, not only in the minds of the good ladies but also in my own mind. Jim had been in the community a full year before I turned up, and he seemed to have had no trouble getting along. Everyone appeared to like his easy, relaxed way, a manner I put down to his having been brought up in a small village in Northern Ontario. I thought uneasily that I might be the problem in the partnership.

When I told Jim about the meeting, he said, "Well, better remember to have coffee next time." I said that it hadn't occurred to me that I should have immediately stoked up the stove and *made* coffee for the ladies. Jim, with a twinkle, said, "You're some sociologist not to have noticed that coffee is always the drink of choice for women in this town. The men probably prefer something stronger."

"I've got to stop assuming my way of doing things is the way they are done here," I replied. "Trouble is, I don't know when I'm doing it, until I've said or done the wrong thing. It's going to take me a while to get used to things. But we *are* in a bit of a cultural desert."

"Well," Jim said, "we'll have to figure out how to make the desert bloom. We'll have to create some kind of oasis or you won't be happy. We've lots of books between us. Some might be of interest. What do you think that lady would like to read?"

"I'd be scared to ask her in case we didn't have anything she'd want. Maybe though, we can figure out how to have some kind of library."

"Maybe we could. But it would have to be open to the whole town and the farming community. When Jesus fed the multitude with the two loaves and the five fishes he didn't do it because he wanted everyone to turn up at the synagogue on Saturday. He did it because they were hungry. A library would have to be open to everybody, whether they go to our church, some other, or none. It's too bad there's no office in the church."

"Even if there was," I said, "people who never come to church might hesitate to come to our library."

"Not unless they were coming to get married, buried, or asking to have their child 'done.' But you know, I've been thinking for some time about trying to find some place to have an office downtown. The church budget will never cover it, but the Georges, who run the part-time telephone exchange, rent their front room to an Edmonton lawyer who hardly ever uses it. Think I'll get in touch with him and see if we can figure something out. Think his name is McPherson."

Jim contacted McPherson, who said he was using his office less and less, and would be glad to let Jim use it. He could also use the lawyer's Underwood typewriter and desk. His father had been a Methodist circuit rider, and he well understood the problems of a rural parish. So now Jim had a well-equipped downtown office. He was delighted that he no longer had to handwrite his sermons, church business letters, or his weekly column for the *Mayerthorpe Review*. The office also provided a neutral place on the main street where people could feel free to come regardless of church affiliation.

Before we got around to establishing the library, the benefits of an office in the heart of the business district were soon evident. If business was slow, merchants or their clerks would drop in to chat. Location in the telephone exchange building provided another benefit. Mrs. George, who had to manually plug in every call, operated it. If she happened to overhear someone talking to a friend about needing to get a ride into Edmonton, she would break into the conversation and tell the caller who was going. She was never known to spread gossip and was highly regarded as a helpful source of information. If she picked up information she thought Jim ought to know about—a road accident, an emergency trip to the hospital, or a sudden death— she'd rush into his office to tell him. The downtown office meant that nothing of concern happened in the village, or the wider community, that Jim didn't hear about almost immediately.

Having secured an office, we then thought about how to establish a library. One of Jim's parishioners, the wife of an English remittance man living on an isolated farm in the Greencourt area, had told Jim she'd longed for something to read when she first immigrated. She found she could get a box of books mailed to her on loan every month from the Extension Department of the University of

Alberta in Edmonton. She thought there was no reason that Jim couldn't do the same. Jim applied, and the boxes began to come.

After getting a couple more orange crates from the Co-op, and adding a number of our own books, the library was opened. True, only a small handful of eager readers actually borrowed books. But we left *Decline of the West* safely hidden on a bottom shelf at home. Thankfully, no one asked for it.

five

Money Back Guaranteed

Growing up during the Depression, I was used to living on very little money, always making my own clothes, rarely going to the movies or the theatre, never eating out, and saving every penny. Poverty seemed almost a professional requirement of ministry, lest riches sully the work of serving the Lord. I was not daunted by the prospect of marrying a United Church minister with an annual salary of $1,800.

However, when Jim and I sat down to figure out our first budget some months before the wedding, it was clear that a number of things—such as books, magazines, doctor, insurance, and holidays—could not be accommodated. Nor could my mother's admonition, given frequently in my childhood: "Margaret, never marry a man who won't give you your own money to spend!" Jim suggested that if we cut our food budget by three dollars a month, I could have a spending allowance, but we both knew it was an imaginary figure.

"But what the heck," Jim said. "Ministers always turn their wedding fees over to their wives. Maybe I'll have a lot of weddings. I already have a car, so we're all set."

The pastoral charge came with a furnished manse, owned and maintained by the church through teas, fowl suppers, and bazaars organized by the Ladies' Aid. And in those years, no minister's family ever received a bill from the doctor, who had himself been a son of the manse, brought up to selflessly serve suffering humanity.

Not long after our arrival in Mayerthorpe, I began to have a gnawing pain in my lower right abdomen. Since the village's only doctor had just left and a new one had not arrived, we had to climb into Huh! and drive ninety miles along the barely gravelled highway to Edmonton, a journey that took at least four hours—more if it rained and you got caught in gumbo. The diagnosis was made in a matter of minutes; I had a growth on my right ovary the size of a lemon. I would have to have it removed as soon as arrangements could be made for a bed and a surgeon. We chugged home and a few days later got a call asking me to register the next day at the Royal Alexandra Hospital.

I wasn't worried about the operation or the outcome. My mother had been a nurse and always treated illness with a businesslike calm. In those days, you relied entirely on what the doctor said, followed his orders, and got on with getting better, which in my experience you always did. So I was almost nonchalant as we took off: a few days, maybe a week, without a ringing phone or a knock at the door. Wonderful! I think my nonchalance rubbed off on Jim, because he agreed not to make the long trip to visit me but instead to ask our Edmonton friends to check on me and let him know.

When I came to after the operation, I found myself in a room with another patient, Kathie Simpson. She told me she'd been operated on three days before and hoped to get home to Red Deer soon, but her doctor wanted her to stay for at least another week. She said she felt as if she had spent most of her life in hospitals; this had been her tenth operation. Later that day, a woman breezed into the room. "Mrs. Simpson," she said, "I'm the comptroller from the finance office. When you were admitted a few days ago, they were very busy with patients from a bus accident, and so they didn't get all your financial information. I need your husband's name, occupation, and salary."

Kathie said her husband's name was Larry. "But he's just changed his job and I don't know what his salary is. Anyway, he never tells me things like that."

"Well, what is he doing now?"

"He's working as a salesman in the dry-goods department of Woodward's."

"What we really need to know is how you are planning to pay for your stay in the hospital."

Kathie said she didn't know, she'd have to ask her husband.

"This is a very expensive room. If you don't know how you're going to pay for it, you'll have to move to the public ward."

"But my doctor said I must be in a semi-private room. He ordered my husband to make sure I got one."

"Doctors have no business ordering semi-private rooms. They don't pay the patients' bills. So you better get in touch with your husband as soon as possible." With that she flounced out.

That night, Kathie had nightmares. She cried and thrashed about so much that they had to put bars on the sides of her bed to make sure she didn't fall out. She kept talking to her husband in her sleep. "Oh Larry, I'm so sorry. I didn't mean to be sick again. I'll get a job as soon as I get out. Somehow I'll find a job and I'll pay back all the money you've spent on me. Honest I will. I won't ever get sick again. Oh Larry, I'm sorry I've been so much trouble to you. Please forgive me."

I was close to tears myself, listening to all this, and angry at the heartless way in which Kathie had been spoken to. While I tossed and turned, worrying about Kathie, I suddenly thought, "Gosh, they didn't ask Jim what his salary was! Just as well, since we're two months behind in getting paid, and Jim hasn't had any weddings since we arrived, not that they would have helped much. I bet that old moneybags will come and see me tomorrow."

She did, but I was prepared. "Mrs. Norquay, they didn't get all the information we need. We have to know how you are planning to pay for this room."

"Well, I don't really know. But we've always managed so far to pay our bills, so I guess we'll figure it out."

"You'll have to figure it out as soon as possible and let us know. This is an expensive room."

"Well, if we can't manage to pay by the time the doctor says I can go home," I said, "I guess you'll just have to keep me here in the hospital until we can."

She swallowed, coughed harshly as if stricken by something caught in her throat, and left the room.

The next day a letter arrived from my mother. "Your father says not to worry about hospital bills. Like Eaton's," she wrote, "we always guarantee our product."

six

No Hornets Here

A few weeks after we arrived in Mayerthorpe, the Co-op called its annual meeting. Jim had been a member of the Co-op ever since he had arrived the previous year. According to custom, a man's membership automatically made his wife eligible to attend. The Mayerthorpe Co-op was owned by its members, most of whom were farmers from the surrounding community, a radius of some fifty miles. It was a kind of general store, featuring groceries, canned goods, a few locally grown root vegetables, and miscellaneous household needs such as Dutch Cleanser, toilet paper, corn brooms, fly swatters, some farm supplies, rubber boots, overalls, and chicken feed. I'd never belonged to a co-op before, but working with *Farm Radio Forum* (a national radio program for farmers) in my first job after university, I had been involved in organizing a county firefighting co-op and was keen to see how another kind of co-op worked. When we got to the hall, there were about two hundred people there, most of them men, though a fair number had brought their wives.

The meeting began with financial reports for the last year of operation and a presentation of next year's budget outlining the projected expenditures and hoped-for profit—which in the co-op tradition would be returned to its members in proportion to the amount of money they had spent in the store. This amount would not be finalized until the accounts had been audited, but the prospect of getting some money back at the end of the year was of considerable interest.

When they got to estimating next year's profit, Harold Stubbins got to his feet and asked why the Co-op was no longer carrying womens' lingerie. The Board chair called on the manager to explain. He said that they had recently enrolled in the Alberta Co-op Wholesale Management program and the Wholesale had advised against carrying womens' lingerie because it was perishable —as bad as bananas. It went out of style quickly, and if it didn't sell they could suffer a serious loss. The Wholesale's advice was costing $900 a year, and it was too much to pay for advice if they didn't use it. Lingerie never sold very fast, so they had to keep it on display all the time to remind people they carried it. When they were moving flour and grain bags around, it often got dusty and then they'd have to reduce the price just to get rid of it. Harold said, "People have been able to get lingerie at the Co-op for years and it'll be really inconvenient for a lot of folks if they can't get it."

Joey Stokes got up and said, "My wife always buys her underwear from Eaton's catalogue, and she says you have a lot more choice."

Harold said Eaton's was too expensive.

Joey said people could always go to Harrison's (the village dry-goods store). "But I've heard they're considering going into groceries and that'll put the Co-op out of business. Better leave the ladies' underwear to them."

Harold said, "But Harrison's lingerie has no sense of style."

This discussion was a bit too much, and I got up and said I didn't understand why a man was making such a fuss over women's lingerie. Did he have a special reason for needing to buy it? I thought we ought to take Alberta Wholesale's advice, since we'd already paid for it, and then if our profits went down we could do something different next year.

My comment was greeted with great applause, and when the call came for nominations to the Board, though no women had previously taken part in any discussion, two farmers' wives leapt to their feet, one to nominate me, and the other to second the motion. I tried to decline, saying I was too new in town to become a Board member. I didn't know enough yet about the community to be of use. I'd been brought up in farming country, and knew that newcomers can easily and innocently get into a hornet's nest if they do anything too soon, before they know the score. The chair said, "We all get along in Mayerthorpe. You won't have any trouble in our village and anyway we never have hornets. The weather's too cold." He added that since I came from the East I would doubtless have some experience that could be helpful. I'd always thought the East was the Orient, but after a week in Mayerthorpe I'd discovered that in Alberta, the East is Ontario. The chair made me feel that if I didn't agree to let my name stand I'd be like every other Easterner who turned up—had things to say but wouldn't stay to help. They just bided their time until they could move back East. I reluctantly agreed to let my name be added to the already prepared totally-male slate, which was then elected unanimously.

The chairman of the Board announced that at the end of the meeting he'd like all Board members to remain to set up a meeting schedule. So I stayed behind and sat at one end of the semicircle of twelve chairs the chairman had set out. The meeting began with the chairman counting out loud to twelve. He then said, "There's someone missing," and counted again. "Someone's missing." There was a bit of a pause then he said, "Oh! I didn't count you, Mrs. Norquay." And so my dubious career as a Board member of the Mayerthorpe Co-op began.

I happened the next day to drop into Harrison's to pick up material for some sewing I was doing. The high school boy who belonged to our young people's group and worked there part-time said, "Oh, Mrs. Norquay, I hear you're going to help make the Co-op store respectable." It was my first lesson in how fast news travels in Mayerthorpe. I began to think that perhaps Mayerthorpe did have hornets.

seven

Mr. Kringsberg's Christmas Dinner

The year Christmas Day fell on a Sunday, there was frost on the inside of the front door when we wakened, and the thermometer outside the kitchen window registered thirty below. We always got up early on Sundays, never knowing what the day might bring, for the roads were always unpredictable. We had to hurry, because Jim had a service to conduct in a small community eleven miles north of the village. Huh! always needed special attention in winter. The radiator, routinely drained at night, had to be refilled, and the engine warmed enough to encourage Huh! to start. The ashes left in the stove were still hot that morning, so Jim put the ashpan under the engine, hoping that when we were ready to leave, Huh! would agree to take off. On this day it did.

There were seven preaching points on Jim's charge, some of them remote communities that had services only one Sunday a month. People in outlying areas lived in relative isolation: the farms were large, strung out along ungravelled roads where Alberta Telephone had not yet ventured. Connor Creek was one such community. It was the turn of that congregation to have a service on Christmas morning. The Connor Creek area began at the end of a dirt road about eleven miles north of Mayerthorpe. The physical centre of the community and its only visible symbol was the one-room schoolhouse, which the impersonal process of consolidation had long since caused to be abandoned. The school was run down, the building shabby with peeling paint and broken windowpanes. It was here that the tiny congregation of three or four families met once a month on Sundays for worship and fellowship. The services afforded the only remaining opportunity for the community to get together. And we knew the whole congregation would be there for the service on Christmas Day.

We left early because the snow had fallen deep in the night, and despite the stability of the Model A, we thought the driving might be treacherous. It was doubtful that anyone would get to the school ahead of time to light the fire in the old airtight heater and we knew there was little chance of our getting the place reasonably comfortable with so many broken windows. But we planned to arrive early and do what we could. It seemed too bad that on Christmas Day, of all days, the congregation should have to stand huddled around an airtight heater, scorching the fronts of their coats and half freezing their backs.

When we drove up to the school we saw a large handwritten sign nailed to the door:

> **This Here is Too Cold**
> **Come to My Place**
> **Signed**
> **A. Kringsberg**

A. Kringsberg, whose first name we never knew, was a bachelor, an old-age pensioner badly crippled with arthritis, who lived by himself a mile away in a long, narrow dwelling made of three old granaries nailed together. His pension was his sole means of support, and the monthly gathering of the congregation was one of the few joys of his life. We chugged down the road again, and soon saw his house nestled in deep snow against a tall stand of trees, with smoke pouring black out of the stovepipe chimney. When he opened the door, a mass of hot air rushed to greet us. He shook us warmly by the hand and said, "Merry Christmas! Merry Christmas! I've been looking forward to this day all year."

When our eyes, blinded by the glare of the snow, became accustomed to the light inside, we saw to our astonishment that he had transformed the room into a kind of chapel. There were four sturdy benches made of fresh-hewn pine a foot wide and two inches thick. He had nailed three apple boxes together for a pulpit, and over the top had folded a worn, wrinkled, but spotless white damask cloth, which he had obviously laundered himself. The old man told us that he had realized some months before that Connor Creek's December service would fall on Christmas Day. He knew that the school would be impossible to heat, and without telling anyone he made plans of his own. He had walked twelve miles to the Mayerthorpe lumberyard, got planks cut to his specifications, and had them trucked out. In his own woodlot he had cut the logs to make the supports.

He led us to a second room to remove our coats and warm our hands at the old cookstove, whose top was almost red hot and whose kettle was boiling at a furious rate. In a few moments, we heard sleigh bells and shouts of laughter. We looked out to see a large sleigh drawn by two horses, loaded with assorted children and adults wearing bright Christmas mittens and scarves. As the sleigh unloaded, a couple of farm trucks drove up, and soon everyone was inside, shouting "Merry Christmas" and shaking hands all round. In a few minutes the congregation of nineteen persons was seated and the service began.

As the traditional scripture was read and the familiar carols were sung, we could hear the wood crackling loudly in the stove, flames roaring dangerously up the stovepipe, and the hiss of the kettle, which Mr. Kringsberg kept refilling. It seemed strangely appropriate that the birthday of a Babe born in a stable should be celebrated in a weather-beaten old granary. When the benediction had been pronounced, the children began tugging at their parents to start for home to open their presents and eat the Christmas dinner left cooking in the oven. But before anyone could make a move to put on a coat, Mr. Kringsberg said, "Now you must all stay and have lunch. The kettle is boiling and I have bread for sandwiches and milk for the children."

The women exchanged brief glances, each thinking of the turkey that might burn if not attended to, or the expected guests who might arrive and find no one home. Without anyone saying a word, each realized that this was Mr. Kringsberg's Christmas gift to the community. It was his Christmas dinner, perhaps the only one he would have. Thanking him for his thoughtfulness, the women went to the second room, which served as a kitchen, and made an enormous pile of salmon sandwiches.

The white cloth was opened full out to cover the rough wooden table, the tea was brewed, the milk poured. Thanks were spoken and we all sat down to eat. When all the tea had been drunk, the sandwiches eaten, and folks were getting ready to excuse themselves to leave, Mr. Kringsberg rose to his feet. "And now I have a special surprise for the children." With that, he hobbled to a cupboard, and after much rustling of paper and moving of boxes he emerged carrying a large dinner plate in each hand. On one was a huge pile of yellow marshmallow cookies and on the other an identical pile of pink ones. The children were overjoyed. This was the grand climax every feast should have. But as their parents watched the cookies being gleefully demolished, they wondered silently how many meals the old man might have had to go without to provide what he had given us all that day.

When at last it was time to go, several expressed concern that Mr. Kringsberg was apparently planning to spend the rest of the day alone rather than go to his neighbour's as he had done in former years. He gently refused any invitation, saying only that all his life he had wanted to give a Christmas dinner but had never before had anyone to invite. But now he had done it. He was tired and would stay home and listen to classical music on the CBC. He hoped we all would have a joyful day.

When we drove away, we felt we had been warmed and fed as never before. We knew the Birthday Child would be well pleased with the dinner Mr. Kringsberg had given.

eight

In a Pinch, Use Tarpaper

We had just finished our coffee and listened to the eight o'clock news when Jim pulled back his chair and said, "Monday is supposed to be my day off, and by gosh this time I'm going to take it. I've still got my column to write for the *Mayerthorpe Review*, and I'm supposed to go to Cy Philips Hardware this morning to meet with the businessmen who want me to help them plan a skating carnival for next winter. I think I can let the column wait a bit—I'll do it tonight. I'll phone Cy and tell him I won't be at his meeting because I've something more pressing I have to do." Putting down the phone, he said he didn't know anything about skating carnivals. Sometimes he wished people taking on a new project wouldn't always assume that he'd know how to do it because he came from the East. "I want to go to Surprise Lake and find out whether Whitecourt Lumber has delivered the siding they promised for the cookhouse. I need it within a couple of weeks so we can start building as soon as seeding is finished." The building was intended for what Jim hoped would mark the beginning of a permanent summer camp for children—a project Jim had dreamed about ever since he'd come to Mayerthorpe.

The previous summer, we'd taken our holidays camping on the lake, exploring it in a fragile birchbark canoe lent to us by a man whose Indian grandfather had made it. The canoe was so fragile it bulged in the middle, making me want to stop paddling and look back and check to see if Jim was still coming. By the time we circled the lake and landed safely ashore, we assured ourselves that the site was, indeed, a perfect place for a children's camp.

I jumped at the chance for an all-day outing to Surprise Lake. I made a quick lunch of sandwiches, filled a Thermos, and we were off.

A children's camp was something relatively rare in Alberta at the time, and non-existent within a hundred miles north and west of

Edmonton. Jim and I had both experienced the delights of going to camp as children, and later working as camp counsellors, and knew well the many benefits that could ensue. I shared heartily in Jim's dream.

When we got to the site, we saw that the wood siding had arrived, and for a few moments we just revelled in the beauty of the place. It was a jewel of a little lake, set on several acres of Crown land, with no sign of human habitation. Except for a narrow bit of sand beach, the whole perfect circle of it was marked out by trees whose branches were blossoming into a soft, lacy green, shimmering in the May sun. On the far side was a small tree-covered island, its green lace reflected in the water.

We didn't linger over lunch because Jim was anxious to map out the site. He'd asked for enough siding to build a three-walled structure about twenty-four feet long and twelve wide, open at the front. He thought he could wall in sleeping quarters for the cook at one end, leaving enough room for a cookstove and supplies and providing shelter for fifteen to twenty boys to eat, should it rain. He and the campers would sleep in tents. He checked out the siding, which was, as he expected, full of knotholes and cracks, it being a donation of third-grade lumber. Whitecourt had sent studding for the whole structure, siding for the walls, but nothing for the roof. That would be a problem for another day. Today, Jim wanted to put in stakes, marking where the shelter would stand, so that the building could start once spring seeding was finished and he could get some volunteers from the farming community to help. Most farmers would be able to help for only a day or two, but the shelter would have to be finished before haying started. He was planning one experimental camp for the middle of July, hoping for an enthusiastic response, which might engender support for something better.

After he'd staked out the place for the building, he thought he'd better figure out where to put a makeshift outhouse. Every time we passed a government picnic site in the last year, we checked out the biffies and thought we'd found an ideal design that would keep out flies but let light in with the door shut, and have enough screened windows so it wouldn't smell. Jim was sure there wouldn't be time or money to build one this year, so they'd have to make do with a log, a trench, and pails of ashes from the campfire and the cookstove. So we looked for a clearing that would allow for an eight-foot log and trench.

That done, Jim thought we ought to take a walk around the lake and explore the shoreline.

We did hear a few distant rumbles of thunder as we started out, but there wasn't a cloud in the blue Alberta sky. We were anxious to confirm our opinion that the site would be a good place to have a camp. Putting on our rubber boots, we started off to circle the lake. We walked over moss-covered logs, jumped and stumbled over patches of marsh, speculated about what we could do with the bark that had fallen off old birch trees, and admired an aspen so festooned with old man's beard that we could hardly see the trunk. We didn't give a thought to the weather. Suddenly it began to rain—in a few minutes we had a cloudburst. We stumbled back over the uneven terrain as fast as we could, having no idea how much time had elapsed since we'd left the campsite. Getting wet was the least of our concerns. Too much rain, and Huh! might get caught in gumbo when we drove out. The road had been slightly damp when we'd driven in.

Jim figured it took us about an hour and a half to reach the car. Soaking wet, we jumped in and Jim started the engine. Someone with a large truck had driven out before us, and the road was deeply rutted. We drove a couple of yards, Jim carefully accelerating and breaking, when Huh! refused to go farther. It was time to get the shovel. Jim stopped the engine and got out of the car. Unfortunately, he hadn't yet changed his aluminum snow shovel for his garden spade, and the snow shovel crumpled on his first attempt to load it with wet mud. Nothing to do now but push. Jim put the engine back in gear, I got out, and we both pushed. In a few minutes the car started off by itself. We tried to run after it, but the exertions of pushing in the gumbo had mired our boots, and neither of us could lift a foot. The only thing to do was to get out of the boots, take our socks off and walk in bare feet, which we knew from experience didn't stick to gumbo. It was easy enough to get out of our boots, but it took several strong sustained tugs to get the boots out of the gumbo, which finally released them with a loud sucking noise. By this time, the engine had sputtered and Huh! had stopped. As we walked to the car, a boot and sock in each hand, the rain stopped and the sun came out.

The road ahead was even more badly rutted, as if someone had tried to drive in from the highway, got stuck, and been towed out by a large truck. We climbed into Huh!, hung our boots and socks to dry over the side mirrors, and decided we'd better wait until help came along. We sat there with the doors open so our feet would dry, and in about an hour we heard a tractor coming from behind us. It stopped when it got to us. "Yer stuck, are yuz? Maybe I can help yuh."

The driver grabbed his tow rope and jumped out. "Quite a car yuh got there. Haven't seen one like that in years. Nobody comes along this road unless they're comin' to my farm. So what in tarnation brought yuh here?"

"I'm James Norquay, the United Church minister from Mayerthorpe. I'm going to build a children's camp here on the lake. I came to find out if the lumber Whitecourt promised us had got here."

"Yeah, they came in a couple of days ago. They got stuck, too, and I had to give 'em a tow. Why didn't they give you some good stuff? That lumber won't build you much."

Jim said, "It's only a shelter for the cookhouse, and for the kids to eat in, if it rains. We're going to sleep in tents."

"Tents! Who'd ever want to sleep in tents? Most 'round here had enough livin' in tents when we cleared the land to start the farm and build the house."

"I took three or four boys camping a couple of years ago at Moonlight Bay, just outside Edmonton, and they all want to do it again and bring all their friends. But we need some place a bit nearer than Edmonton. So we're planning to build a camp here. Trouble is, I've got enough siding for the walls, but nothing but the studding for the roof."

"Reverend, yuh need more than studding. I took a lot of timber out of my woodlot this winter and I've lots of log slabs left—more'n I need—and there's more where they came from. You can have enough of 'em to cover the studding, and I'll truck 'em to the campsite. But they won't fit solid. You'll need sumpin' to cover 'em."

"Yes, but I haven't figured that out yet."

"Well, Reverend, I tell yuh, go into Edson and see Carson Jabbers at the Hardware and Farm Supply. Tell Carson that Jake Kronski sent yuh and he's to help yuh out and give yuh a good price. I buys all my binder twine, chicken feed, chainsaw blades, darn near everything from him. So he'll help yuh. But now, let's get yuh to the highway."

When we got to the highway, Jim thought if we went right to Edson we could probably reach the Hardware and Farm Supply before it closed. When Jim told Carson Jabbers that Jake Kronski had sent him, Carson responded with a smile. "I always takes my orders from Jake. The only thing I've got that you could use to cover the slabs is tarpaper. If yuh put it on double it might last two, three years. You can have it for what I paid for it—a dollar a roll. Yuh'll need about eight rolls."

"Sold!" Jim said, and asked if he could pick it up when he came with a crew to build the shelter.

"Sure! Come when it's convenient. I'll still be here."

We started off for home, trying to figure out what to do if the Mayerthorpe church wasn't able to make up the deficit on Jim's last-month's salary. If not, would we have enough money to buy the rolls of tarpaper, the nails, a used cookstove and food supplies for at least a dozen hungry boys? I remembered there were a few dollars left in my bank account (still in my maiden name) from the last paycheque I got before I was married. And there was a bit more in our donation jar from Jim's wedding fees, which traditionally were given to the minister's wife. I'd kept it all for a rainy day. Well, I thought, we've sure had a rainy day.

nine

Sweet Singing in the Choir

I had just brought in a load of kindling to restart the stove and heat the water for the week's washing when a knock came to the front door. It was a man I'd never seen before, but he introduced himself as Tom Harrison, the piano tuner. He said he came out from Edmonton once a year to tune all the town's pianos. "I wondered if you folks have a piano you'd like tuned."

"Yes, we do have a piano, but for goodness sakes come in, Mr. Harrison. It was thirty-five below this morning when we got up, and that wind is devastating."

He insisted on taking off his boots before he crossed the threshold, so while I held the door, I explained that my mother-in-law thought all her children should have a piano, and about a year and half ago she'd sent us money for a second-hand one. "We bought an old Nordmeyer and had it trucked out from Edmonton. I'd be surprised if it doesn't need tuning. I'm not sure it had been properly tuned when we bought it. So I'd love to have you tune it."

While Mr. Harrison tuned the piano, I restarted the stove, thinking I could at least offer him a cup of tea and a bowl of soup when he finished. The washing could wait. The piano tuned, Mr. Harrison said some soup to warm him up before his next call would be great, and so we had a bit of a talk over the soup. He said, "It is remarkable that in a town of slightly over 400 people, there are more than fifty pianos. Everybody doesn't have their piano tuned every year, though they should—but enough people do that it's worth my while to come."

"How'd we come to have so many pianos?" I asked.

"Well, it's because of Mrs. Simpson."

"Who is Mrs. Simpson?"

"She's the piano teacher. She's a graduate of the Leningrad Conservatory, and she married a retired English sea captain who bought a farm here. He wasn't much of a farmer, and died within a couple of years. So Mrs. Simpson moved into town, and she earns her living teaching music. She's been at it for at least ten years. I'm not bad on the violin, and I look forward to coming every year because on the day I tune Mrs. Simpson's piano she invites me to dinner and then we spend the evening playing together. It's great because I don't have anyone to accompany me in Edmonton, and Mrs. Simpson doesn't have anybody here who likes classical music to accompany her or to play with."

To find out we had such a person as Mrs. Simpson in town was wonderful news. For some time I'd thought of organizing a children's choir, but I wasn't sure I could work with Mrs. McCallian, our church organist. She did the best she could but had serious limitations reading music and almost always faked the bass line in the hymns. Once, when she was mad at Jim because she didn't like the hymns he'd picked for a service, she defiantly changed "Jesus Lover of My Soul" from the minor key to the major.

If Mrs. Simpson had been teaching piano for ten years, she might have a senior student who could accompany a children's choir. Mr. Harrison said I should talk to her. He was sure she'd want to help.

I'd had a few piano lessons as a child and had sung in choirs all my life, but still I was a bit daunted approaching Mrs. Simpson. I needn't have worried. She was delighted to hear about a children's choir. There were no music teachers in the schools, and judging by the presentations at the annual music festival, it was apparent that few teachers could read music. Except for her piano students, there were no opportunities for the children to experience the joys of music. She had a senior pupil she was sure was skilled enough to accompany the choir, and she thought the girl would jump at the chance. Thus encouraged, and knowing I was protected by the myth that anyone from the East could do anything, I decided to go ahead with the choir. But as a kind of insurance, I sent for a book on teaching children to sing.

There was only one problem. Would Mrs. McCallian be offended that we hadn't asked her? The church had never had a children's choir, and the adult choir she'd pulled together had fallen apart shortly after we arrived. Jim thought the best way to handle it was to make it clear that while the choir might sing at church services, it was intended to serve the whole community. In his next column for the *Mayerthorpe Review*, a notice appeared, announcing the formation of a choir for children from seven to fourteen.

"Children whose parents are not affiliated with the United Church, and who wish to have the experience of singing in a choir, are welcome to attend practice and participate in secular programs with no obligation to sing at services. No child will be excluded because he can't keep a tune. The only requirement is to attend practise every Thursday after school. There will be an annual fee of fifty cents to help buy the music, but the fee can be paid in instalments."

About thirty-five children showed up the first week. Everyone could sing except for six little boys, five seven-year olds and one nine, who sang in a monotone. I didn't exactly tell them they weren't ready to sing in a choir, but told them they wouldn't need to come on Thursdays if they would come to the manse on another day, once a week, after school. Then I would give them some special lessons all by themselves. They were delighted and all agreed to come. Mrs. Simpson's pupil, Eva Harris, a sixteen-year-old high school girl, was able to master the church pump organ after three or four practices, and seemed to enjoy the experience. Half the choir could read music, so, beginning with rounds and canons, it wasn't long before they could all sing in parts.

Getting the little monotones to sing in tune was a different experience. It involved working with each child individually. First I tried to find the note on the piano closest to the one they were voicing—usually about middle C. I'd strike the key, ask the child to listen hard, and then try to match his sound with the piano. Once a child got middle C right, I'd say, "Bingo! You've got it," and we'd all clap. Someone else would take a turn, and we'd go through the same procedure. Once middle C was right on the first try each week, I'd move up to D or down to B depending on what seemed easiest for the particular child. Once the boys caught on to the low notes, I concentrated on keys above C, trying to help them find their soprano head tones. Occasionally, I'd have to stop an argument about who took the fewest number of tries to get a note right. However, the boys never failed to turn up, and bragged to their schoolmates who weren't in the choir that they'd been chosen to get special singing lessons. Soon they all began to get restless, insisting they wanted to sing a tune. I said we already knew enough notes to sing the first line of a song I knew, but we needed three more notes to sing the whole song. Johnnie Gertson, one of the seven-year-olds, asked, "Couldn't we sing the first line?" Then a chorus of "Please, please let us sing the first line," so I sang the first line of "Twinkle, Twinkle, Little Star."

Nine-year-old Billy Durham said, "That's a baby song. I don't want to sing that."

"It is not a baby song," Johnnie said. "My mother sings it with me and I'm seven."

I intervened at that point and said as soon as they could sing the whole verse and had found their soprano voices they could sing with the choir.

We got to the whole verse in another couple of weeks, but they were still straining and singing in their lower register. So I said we were now going to work on some *really* high notes, and sang a scale to model the change in voicing. Then, saying "Listen to this," I played the B above middle C and then the C at the top of the scale. Johnnie instantly matched them both, with the most beautiful soprano tone. He looked surprised, and the boys all clapped.

I said, "Johnnie hang on to it. Try and remember how it feels. Can you do it again?"

He could! Within another couple of weeks they all could do it, and with great glee turned up proudly at the Thursday practice. Two years later, Johnnie sang a solo at the Easter service.

ten

Nobody Asked Me
to Buy a Ticket

I had just got back from an interminable community meeting, in a great rush to have dinner ready the minute Jim got home. I knew he had to get away for an early meeting with the church Board. There was a knock on the door, and there stood two smiling children from my junior church choir. "Mrs. Norquay, the Anglican Ladies' Association are raffling a bride doll and we thought you'd like a chance to win it. So we came to see you right away. The draw will be made at their bake sale, on the Saturday after Remembrance Day. The tickets are three dollars each, or two for five."

I took a deep breath—what to do? How could I disappoint these children who faithfully turned up to choir practice every Thursday? How could I explain that it was against our family policy, and the policy of the United Church, to participate in raffles? I'd been brought up to believe that gambling was a mortal sin, but I'd long ago decided that there were other sins more worthy of eternal damnation, like hurting your neighbour or stealing your friend's wife. However, I was bound by the official policy of the United Church. These two children were regular members of my choir, but they were never allowed to sing with us on Sunday because they had to go to their own church. They'd been embarrassed when their mother wouldn't let them sell tickets for the choir's annual concert, held to raise money for choir gowns. It was as if they were trying to make it up to me by offering a chance at the doll. So I pulled five dollars out of our donation cookie jar and rushed back to make dinner.

A month later, on November 11, a Remembrance Day service was held in the town hall for the whole community. The Anglican priest had conducted the service the previous year. This time it was my husband's turn. In addition to the usual comments about how Canadian soldiers had given their lives for their country, Jim felt moved to express his disappointment that the room above the pool hall was being used regularly for gambling—for poker games. He said that he was particularly saddened to know that the games had been organized by the town merchants, most of whom were veterans of the First World War. They were setting a bad example and had already caused hardship to some young families whose fathers, veterans of the Second World War, were having trouble paying gambling debts. The older veterans should be setting an example. Was this the country they had fought for?

The Saturday of the draw, we couldn't go to the Anglican Ladies' bake sale because we were expected at our closest neighbouring church, the United Church in Sangudo, a few miles down the highway. When we got home about 5:30, I realized we were out of bread and dashed to the bakery, hoping it would still be open. When I entered, Mrs. Climie greeted me with a broad smile. "Mrs. Norquay, congratulations! I hear you've won the bride doll!"

My heart sank. Downtown Saturday in Mayerthorpe, news travels at the speed of light. I rushed out, almost running down the street toward the manse, only to meet two of the Anglican ladies coming from the other direction. One said, "We just dropped the doll off at your house, Mrs. Norquay. We hope you enjoy it."

Not a chance, I thought. When I got in, Jim was sitting in his easy chair, staring at the doll ensconced on the living-room couch. There she was—an Eaton's Beauty Doll, about two feet tall, wearing a long white-satin embroidered dress and veil, obviously made with great care by one of the Anglican ladies, probably Mrs. Jenkins. The bouquet of fabric roses and forget-me-nots would have to have been ordered specially from the Eaton's catalogue.

Jim said, "Where on earth did this come from? I didn't know you still liked to play with dolls."

"I can't imagine what to do with it," I replied. "I just didn't know how to turn down those two Anglican kids from the choir when they came to sell me tickets. It never occurred to me I'd win it, never thought to tell you, and forgot all about it."

"I can understand that, but we're in a bit of a fix. George Thompson, chair of the Board, dropped in to see me this morning at my office. He told me I ought to know that some of the businessmen are very angry about my sermon on Remembrance Day. As manager of the bank, he'd just listened to them and tried to calm them down. But the Legion had called an immediate special meeting, at which some members were reported as saying that I ought to be run out of town. George thought their anger would die down in a couple of days. Of course, you hadn't won the doll when he talked to me. And I had no idea you'd bought a ticket. But with you winning the thing, who knows what will be said about that. I think you'll have to return it."

"Well, I can certainly return lt. I've no use for a doll. Can't even think of anyone I could safely give it to. Trouble is, I don't quite know how to do it without seeming to cast aspersions on the morality of the Anglican Ladies."

"Or the Anglican Church," Jim added.

I anguished over this for some days. I finally returned the doll with a brief note, saying that I was sorry, but for reasons beyond my control, I couldn't accept it. I had bought the tickets because I hadn't wanted to disappoint a couple of the children in my choir. I didn't say they were Anglican children.

The day after the return of the doll, there was a bridal shower to which, as usual, all the women of the community were invited. I didn't attend, but I was told that the story of the doll was the main topic of conversation. It was bad enough that Mrs. Norquay had won the doll—but why did she think she had to give it back? What could they do with it?

Mrs. Jenkins said she would look after it until they figured it out. She'd wrap it in a pillow slip and put it away on the top shelf of her linen closet.

A year later, the Anglican ladies added a going-away outfit for the bride doll, and held another raffle. Nobody offered to sell me a ticket.

eleven

No 911 in the 1950s

I'd been trying for two days to get around to ironing half a dozen of Jim's white shirts, which I'd dampened and rolled for a second time the previous day. I was thankful, however, that unlike most farmers' wives, I didn't have to heat flatirons on the cookstove. But as I set up the ironing board and plugged in the iron, I found myself thinking about our experience with the Fogan family. In trying to get them some help, we'd become painfully aware of how limited resources were for the many social and health problems in the community, for which no one had a ready solution. I had just unrolled my first shirt when I heard a curious noise outside.

I pulled out the iron cord and rushed to the front window, but couldn't see anything because of the trees lining the road. I dashed upstairs and looked out across the farmer's field. A helicopter had landed. A large sled, pulled by a couple of horses, was making its way slowly across the field. When the sled got within a few feet of the helicopter, the door opened and a stretcher carrying a well-wrapped figure was taken out and loaded on the sled, which turned around and started back toward town. At the end of the field, just off the main street, Charlie Bromley, our undertaker, whose panel truck was used both as a hearse and an ambulance, met the sled. The stretcher was moved to the truck, and the truck drove off. I wondered where the stretcher would be taken. To the hospital? Or, oh dear—I didn't want to think.

I rushed downstairs and phoned Jim at his office. I told him I'd just seen a helicopter land in the field across from the house and someone on a stretcher had been taken off. He said, "I don't know exactly what's happened. But an hour ago, Mrs. George came in to tell me that when she plugged the Mayerthorpe hospital phone into Edmonton, she heard them asking for a helicopter, and then heard George Biddle from Anselmo telling Edmonton how to land on his farm. Something about his wife having a baby. He must have come into town on horse-back, because he'd never get his truck through the snow."

"George Biddle! I hope everything is okay. He must have been frozen coming all that way on horseback—sixteen miles."

"Well, that's all I know at the moment," said Jim. "I'll call you when I know more."

I returned to my ironing, worried about what could have hap-pened—and hoping I wouldn't have to wait long before Jim called back. One thing about ironing is that when you've done as much as I have, you can do it almost mindlessly and have the luxury of being free to reflect. I was pregnant with my first child at the time, and as I ironed I found myself wondering what it would be like to have a baby with no doctor and no hospital. An older woman in the congregation had told me she was three years old when she came with her parents in 1905, the year Alberta became a province. She said that when she was growing up, there was a nurse in the community who helped women deliver their babies. The nurse had died a few years previ-ously, but the small log cabin she'd built for this purpose was still in place, the door unlocked as if ready to receive patients.

I went in to see it one day. The birthing room had a single bed, a washstand with a large china bowl and jug, and a small table holding her record book. This book had the names of the mothers, the date of the baby's birth, the weight of the baby, and a notation as to whether the women had paid her or not—the standard rate apparently being one dollar and fifty cents. Our first nurse at Surprise Lake Camp, a woman about forty-five, told me she was born in that cabin in Septem-ber 1915. Her parents had arrived early that summer to begin to clear the land. They'd spent their first winter in a large tent, protected by a surrounding wall of log slabs, in an effort to keep out the worst of the wind and snow. Once the baby arrived, she was kept warm in a lined basket slung with a block and tackle close to the tent roof. I was thankful to be living in a town with both a hospital and a doctor—when was Jim going to phone back?

I finished the first shirt and was on the second when a knock came to my door and a distraught woman I had never seen before asked to come in. She began talking immediately, saying she'd come because her husband was trying to kill her with an axe. "He's trying to cut me up to use for kindling. He wants to kill me. Every morning he puts mouse seed in my porridge. I eat it anyway because I'm healthy. Even if he tries rat poison, it won't kill me. But I can't stand the sight of blood, so I'm afraid of the axe."

Realizing she was probably mentally ill, I gave her a cup of tea to try to calm her down. But she kept on talking wildly, couldn't seem to tell me where she lived, and wouldn't give me her name. She finished the tea, said she had to go, and left. *What if her husband was trying to kill her? Even if I knew where she lived, who was there to call for help? How many things can you worry about at once? We are so bereft of resources in this community.*

The day before, there had been a story in the *Mayerthorpe Review* about a little boy, about two years old, left by himself, locked for several hours in a truck parked on the main street in front of the drugstore. Several passersbys had seen the child and heard his screams but assumed the parents had just dropped into the store to pick up a prescription and would be back in a few moments. John Clackson passed by a second time, several hours later, and was dismayed to find the child still there, now asleep. John thought he would wait until a parent turned up, but decided to go first to the post office, a few minutes away, to pick up the *Edmonton Journal* so he'd have something to read while he waited. He wasn't away more than five minutes, but by the time he got back the truck had left. He hadn't been able to find anyone who knew the owner, and even if he had, what would or could anyone have done about it?

There were no municipal social services, no Children's Aid, not even a service club in Mayerthorpe. There were only the three churches, each staffed by one man who'd never been trained for most of the problems of human need that arrived at the church door. *When oh when is Jim going to call back?*

Another knock at the door. I opened it to find one of our RCMP officers carrying a large brown paper parcel. "Good morning, Mrs. Norquay. We've just confiscated some newly killed moose meat and wondered if you'd like some."

"If it's confiscated, how is it you can give it to us?"

"Well, we're supposed to give it to hospitals, charities, and the aged. You can take your pick."

"I'm not sure which category we fit," I said, "but thanks. Moose meat is great. Jim's brother sometimes sends us some from northern Ontario. I don't know whether hunting moose is illegal there or not. In any case, it wouldn't worry Jim's brother."

"We've already taken the hospital as much as they can use, but we're a bit short on the charities."

"Oh, so *that's* us. Thanks! We'll enjoy it."

I put the meat in the refrigerator and went back to ironing, getting more and more impatient to hear from Jim. George Biddle, the young man who'd given us his granary for the ladies' restroom, was a member of the Anselmo congregation. Was there a baby bundled with that figure on the stretcher? I so hoped everything was all right. I'd just finished the second shirt when Jim called to say all was well. George Biddle had phoned him from the hospital to say that his wife had just delivered a seven-pound baby boy. He was pleased as punch, because it appeared the baby would have red hair, just like his. "He's going to stable his horse and stay in town for the night. I've invited him for dinner and overnight, so maybe you could make up the living-room couch. If you can have dinner ready by six, he'll have time to see his wife this evening, before visiting hours are over. He has to go home tomorrow to look after his cows, but he'll visit with his wife before he goes."

I made up the couch and started to prepare dinner. There would be just enough time to cook the moose. The rest of the shirts could wait.

Next morning, as George was leaving, he said that when the weather cleared in spring, he and his wife would be back to arrange to have their baby "done." Jim went off to his office. I sat down to have another cup of coffee and then got out the ironing board to finish the shirts. This time, the breakfast dishes could wait.

twelve

Don't Tell Your Husband Everything

Sunday afternoon at four o'clock, and the phone was ringing. The exchange was supposed to be closed on Sundays, but Mrs. George must have seen the flash and decided to answer. It was my sister Eleanor, saying she and Don were coming for Christmas from Regina. Wonderful! But how on earth would I manage? We'd been going full stop, organizing Christmas pageants and attending Sunday school concerts, and the house was in a terrible mess. I had no time to clean it up. And our donation jar was empty. I almost wished that I hadn't spent the last fifteen dollars of wedding money on hyacinths to feed the soul—that is, on tickets to the Winnipeg Ballet, which had performed in Edmonton the previous year. Better get a cleaning woman. But was there such a thing in Mayerthorpe? It turned out there was— a single parent with two girls who lived on "the other side of the tracks." I called her and she was pleased to come. I figured I could pay her out of my housekeeping money. I worked along with her, and in the course of our conversation she told me her daughters wanted to sing in the choir. But they hadn't come because they didn't think their clothes were good enough to wear in the choir on Sunday. I was surprised. I hadn't identified what could only be very subtle differences in clothing between people of differing low incomes. All the children had looked the same to me.

I talked it over with Jim and he said the only thing to do was to get choir gowns so all would look the same. An Edmonton firm that made clerical and academic gowns estimated that gowns for thirty-five children between the ages of twelve and eighteen would cost $350. The question was how to raise the money.

In an effort to offer some broad educational opportunities to the community, Jim had earlier applied to become the district representative for the National Film Board. This meant that every month five or six films would arrive that could then be shown to

Huh! on the road

local communities. The only cost was for shipping. Jim planned to make the showings free, but to take up a silver collection and encourage people to contribute whatever they could. Jim thought anything left over could go into the gown fund. The films covered a wide variety of subjects, ranging from cultural full-length features like *The Loon's Necklace* to advice films like *How to Bring Up Your Children*. We did get some flack from a horrified parishioner who objected to a scene where a mother was banging on a potty to entice her two-year-old to use it. But most people appreciated what the films offered.

The high school lent Jim their movie projector and Jim figured out how to run it off Huh!'s battery. This meant he could go to places like Anselmo, to which Alberta Power had not yet extended electricity. By the end of the first year, we had a sum total of $82.45. We had set a goal of having the gowns by Easter of our second year, but still had to raise the rest of the money.

We then planned to organize an amateur night, a popular way to provide local community entertainment and incidentally raise money for a worthy cause. However—not incidentally—we decided to load the show with enough talent that we could sell tickets for fifty cents. To attract people from the surrounding community, we invited a musical saw player from Sangudo who was always pleased to show off his talent, and a woman from Greencourt who was famous for telling jokes. By the end of that evening we had $50.50. How could we raise the rest in the time to get the gowns for Easter?

While I pondered this problem over coffee one morning, the phone rang. It was Mrs. Harrison (two of whose children sang in the choir), who asked me if the choir would come on Christmas Eve and sing carols when people were frantically trying to finish up their shopping. If we'd come, she said, she'd contribute twenty-five dollars to the gown fund. This didn't sit quite right, since Jim had more than once expressed his objections to the commercialization of Christmas. Without consulting him or anyone else, I decided to swallow my scruples and take the choir. In the meantime, a car drove into our driveway. A couple got out, and with no ado, asked us if we would sell them Huh! They wanted it as a wedding present for their son. They could pay $150 for it. It had cost Jim $500, and as an antique might now be worth more. But it had served us well, our parents had recently bought us a new Austin, and we could use the money.

"Sold!" Jim said. We then sent in the order for the gowns. The surplus ($7.95) could go into our donation jar. We could spend it on things the church needed but which the church budget could not support.

thirteen

Best to Hang On
to a Big Jack

It was Easter Sunday, and my children's choir, resplendent in their new choir gowns, had all lined up in the church basement. Half the choir was already up the stairs, waiting to proceed down the aisle, when the organ started up. Our small church was jammed, every chair in use. I'd even seen Bill Woodward, the town handyman. His wife always came to church, but Bill, on the grounds that he was really an Anglican, confined his attendance to once a year, either at Christmas or Easter. *It must be Easter's turn this year,* I thought. Jim was already upstairs making sure there were enough chairs, so everyone would have a place to sit before he began the service.

I was trying to adjust the gown of a straggler who'd come late when the organ began to play and the choir started to move. I heard a slight squeak, like wood being strained. I looked up, and to my horror saw that the ceiling joist was buckling. I barely swallowed a scream. Terrified, I tried to think what to do. In seconds, the choir would be halfway down the centre aisle and the congregation would rise to its feet as one to sing "Jesus Christ Is Risen Today." Would the sudden movement cause the joist to give way? I couldn't think how to stop the organ and the singing to make an announcement without causing panic. Petrified, I thought all I could do was follow the choir and hope the joist would hold. Thank God! Bill Woodward was sitting on the aisle in the back row. I tapped him on the shoulder and beckoned him to follow me downstairs.

"Ah, I can fix that," he said. "I've still got the big jack we borrowed from the hardware when we moved the manse. I was supposed to take it back but never got to it. Think I've a couple of four-by-four timbers in my backyard I can use to shore it up. I'll borrow Ned Nelson's truck to bring it all here. I won't make any noise, and the congregation will never know the difference." I wasn't much reassured, but not knowing what else to do, I rigidly controlled myself so I wouldn't visibly shake and went to sit with the choir.

The congregation got through the first hymn safely and the Scripture readings began. I trembled when the organ started up for the second hymn, but we got through that, too. Should I make some kind of announcement when I got up to conduct the choir's anthem? But how could I do so without causing panic and a stampede? We were all right so far but ... Somehow I managed to get the choir through the anthem, and nine-year-old Johnnie Gertson got to sing his solo. But I was immersed in worry. What if Ned Nelson wasn't home to lend his truck? Was I doing the wrong thing by doing nothing?

The service continued with everyone but me in calm ignorance. In the middle of the third hymn, I thought I heard a couple of slight bumps and there was one more in the middle of the "Amen" at the end. But no one else seemed to have noticed. Halfway through the sermon, to my great relief, I saw Bill come back and sit beside his wife. When the congregation was leaving and everyone was shaking hands with Jim, I heard Jim greet Bill Woodward.

"Great to see you, Bill. I'll look forward to seeing you again next year."

I was glad there'd be a next year.

fourteen

Glad We Didn't Have
Noah's Animals

It was 1953, the third summer that Jim had been building, directing, and running supplies for the boys' camp at Surprise Lake. This year, while Jim was at camp, I was home alone with our new baby, our first child. Unable to get in touch with Jim because the camp had no phone, I began to feel a bit bushed.

When Jim came home to check on us the day the camp closed, I proposed that baby Sara and I go back with him for the week of the Canadian Girls in Training camp, which was being held that year for the first time.

Jim thought it was a great idea. "Sara is growing so fast. I don't want to miss watching her grow. We've got a good staff and you'll only have yourself and Sara to take care of. All the tents are in use, but you can join me in the walled-off corner of the old cookhouse. The roof still seems to be holding out. At least it hasn't leaked yet."

I had a great week and regretted that the girls' camp was closing the next day. Sara still slept most of the day, so I had lots of time to read from the bag of books I'd brought. The weather had been warm, and there'd been no thought of rain. I had easily managed bathing and feeding Sara. I didn't have much washing to do because I had brought disposable diapers, which the Co-op had only recently begun to stock, advertising that they were cheaper than buying water hauled at fifty cents a barrel. There was always warm water in the camp-stove reservoir, and Jim had made a makeshift refrigerator by putting a cooler in a hole in the ground. Banking on continuing warm, dry weather, Jim had eased up on chopping and stockpiling stove wood so he could build another biffy.

About four o'clock on that last afternoon, I had just fed and changed our three-month-old Sara and put her back in her carriage to sleep when I heard a few distant rumblings of thunder. It had been sunny all week. Rain had not been on anyone's mind. But this thunder was disturbing. I looked out the door and saw dark clouds emerging on the far side of the lake. There were soon a few drops of rain and, after a few moments, hail the size of golf balls began to fall, rapidly lowering the temperature. I saw Jim, a large saucepan over his head, dash out of the new kitchen–dining hall and circle the tents to make sure the campers were under cover. Sara began to stir, and I moved the carriage back and forth a few feet, singing her a goodnight song, having changed the words to fit the camp: "Bye, oh baby, bye. Daddy's gone to get firewood, Daddy's gone to get firewood, bye."

The hail lasted a good fifteen minutes and the air got progressively colder, seeping through the cracks and holes in the walls. Finally, dense sheets of rain began to fall. When it briefly subsided, I could hear the counsellors urging the girls to pick up their sleeping bags, empty their tents, and run to the dining hall. My feet were freezing wet on the mud floor. When I realized the hail had poked a hole in the tarpaper roof, I quickly bundled Sara up and followed the campers to the hall, thankful there had been enough time and dry weather between seeding and haying for Jim to have got the hall built. As I went, I could see that the trenches around the tents were all overflowing and one tent had been downed. A current of water ran through the nurse's tent, which served as our first-aid station. It was clear we'd all have to sleep in the dining hall. When I got there, Jim was rushing to bring in a load of wood and the cook was lamenting that she hadn't yet managed to get her fire hot enough to boil the potatoes. She thought supper might be a bit late. It was.

In the meantime, the counsellors made valiant efforts to distract the campers from feeling cold by keeping them occupied with a variety of games. They were aided somewhat by having a baby, now awake, who gurgled and laughed, enjoying all the attention from the girls who took turns talking to and playing with her and were delighted when she smiled. Cookie made sure there was enough meat and vegetables for everyone to have a second helping, and she made a wonderful chocolate cake for dessert. The hot meal seemed to warm everyone up a bit, but we knew our cookstove, despite its fifteen-foot length, still wouldn't heat the place—even if we'd had enough dry wood to keep it going all night, which we didn't. Cookie announced she was going to let her fire burn down to coals; this way she could safely load damp wood into her two large ovens in the hope it would be dry enough in the morning to let her light the fire to make porridge and toast.

Jim and I thought the only thing to do was to keep the girls physically active until they were tired enough to sleep. We'd had an old wind-up gramophone donated, together with some 78-rpm records of country dance music. So, using a scratchy recording of the "Irish Washerwoman," we first taught them a modified version of the Virginia reel, the steps for which are the same for both men and women. When we said we'd teach them a couple of square dances, one of the girls protested loudly that we couldn't do squares because we didn't have any men.

"What's wrong with *me*?" Jim responded. "I've been looking forward all during dinner to doing 'Red River Valley' and 'Listen to the Mockingbird.'"

"But you're only one man." This from a very tall girl, the self-appointed leader.

"Isn't one better than none? Tell you what. You all find yourself a partner, and each time the round changes, you take your turn being the man. We've got enough for four squares, and I'll dance equal time with each square."

"I can't see how that will work," said the same girl.

"Well, I'll dance first with Mrs. Norquay, then I'll take one of you as my partner and you can be the woman. Your partner can dance with Mrs. Norquay, and they can decide who is to be the man. If we dance long enough, you'll all get a chance to dance with me."

"That could take till breakfast."

By this time the other girls were getting impatient, and there was a chorus of "Come on, let's get going, I'm getting cold from standing around."

So we danced until all thirty-two of us were tired out.

The rain slowed enough to let us all go to the biffy, and we climbed into our damp sleeping bags, lying down in rows, happy to be on a dry floor without any tree roots to poke into our backs. Everyone seemed to get to sleep, though I'm sure Sara was the only one who was really comfortable. Warm and cozy in her carriage, which Jim had managed to bring from our sleeping quarters, she hadn't lost her rubber boots, and she didn't know there mightn't be warm water for her bath or that, if we didn't get home the next day, her mother might run out of diapers.

Cookie got up at six, managed to get the fire going, and had breakfast ready by eight. The campers were a bit teary, worrying all through breakfast when, or if, their fathers would arrive to take them home. The lake had risen a foot overnight, and the whole campground was still submerged. Having two years previously discovered the adhesive powers of gumbo on the camp road, we knew no Albertan would attempt to drive that mile in from the highway. If they got to the camp road, they'd leave their cars and walk in. By noon, only seven fathers had turned up. All had come from settlements either on the highway or just off it. No one had managed to get through from outlying areas, where most of the route would have been on dirt roads. By two o'clock, all the staff and most of the campers had gone, and we were sure there would be no more arrivals that day.

Jim and I were left with six girls from the Mayerthorpe district. It was getting colder. There was no more dry wood, food was running out, and most of us were still slightly damp. Jim said we must get out of the camp.

We now had a car, somewhat more powerful than Huh! Our parents, Jim's and mine, worried about Huh!'s inadequacies and had bought us a Baby Austin the previous Christmas. The hail had flattened the ruts in the camp road, and Jim thought if he kept two wheels on the grass at the side, he could probably get out to the highway, as long as he didn't have to stop to meet someone coming the other way. It was worth a try. If he couldn't make it, he'd walk to the highway and thumb his way to Edson to get some help. If he were able to drive out, he'd still have to walk back in, so it might take some time before he'd return.

Miraculously, he was able to drive out. Within an hour and a half he was back to say there would be a couple of cars from Edson parked on the highway at the camp sign. We'd all be taken to Edson, where several families had offered to feed us a hot dinner and keep us overnight if necessary. We should pack our things and make our way. So, loaded with sleeping bags, blanket rolls, suitcases, a small washtub, a diaper pail, and a warmly blanketed baby, we took off in single file, carefully walking on the long grass on the side of the road so as not to get stuck in the gumbo.

As soon as the girls were distributed to Edson homes, Jim got on the phone—only to find that the railway line from Edmonton to Mayerthorpe had been washed out, which meant that the whole area would be impassable. He knew then that none of us would get home that night, and that he'd have to cancel the junior boys' camp that was to come on Monday. After dinner, he spent the rest of the evening on the phone. All the Mayerthorpe girls lived on farms without telephones outside the village. The Mayerthorpe telephone exchange was officially closed after four o'clock on Saturday and all day Sunday, so getting messages to anyone, even indirectly, seemed unlikely. However, since the exchange was in the Georges' house, Mrs. George was known to listen in sometimes when the exchange was closed—especially if the call was from out of town. Jim decided to try to call Charlie Bromely, the Mayerthorpe undertaker, to see if he could bring his panel truck, but Mrs. George's voice came on almost immediately. She said she'd get back to Bromely and would spread the word as well as she could.

Jim then tried to figure out how to get to the staff members and campers who might turn up for camp on Monday. Our Edson hosts helped by giving him the names and phone numbers of people living along the highway east and west of the town, including those at a couple of gas stations and a small truck stop, all of whom, they thought, would try to spread the word.

Wanting to do everything possible to make their guests feel welcome, the host families took the girls to the Saturday-night movie and fed them candy and popcorn, a treat for children who seldom got to movies. The next morning, the hosts took the girls to church, and they were thrilled to be in a "real" church for the first time. Jim spent the morning trying to find out if anybody could get through from Mayerthorpe. Finally the word came that Charlie Bromely, the undertaker, thought his panel truck would be able to make it. He'd have to make a detour to do so, but he thought he could reach Edson by early afternoon.

He was! We packed our car and followed right behind him. Charlie told us later that the girls talked all the way home about what a good time they'd had. They'd been to a real church, with a stained-glass window, and they'd gone to a movie. But best of all, they could brag to their friends that they'd had a ride in the hearse without having to be dead.

fifteen

Never Mess with the WCTU

One day after a Ladies' Aid meeting, a knock came to the back door of the manse. Mrs. Judd-Jones came in, her face tightened and flushed. Without a word of greeting, she cautiously looked into the living room, as if to make sure no one was there, and said in a low voice, "I was cleaning up the kitchen after the Aid's lunch, and found a brown paper bag with five bottles of rum in it. Would you ask Mr. Norquay to investigate when he comes in?"

I said, "Surely it can't be rum, but I'll be glad to tell him when he gets home." Then, unable to control my glee at the thought, I added, "If it's the real thing we'll bring it over and have a party."

The phone rang at that moment, and before I could excuse myself to answer, Mrs. Judd-Jones blinked, pursed her lips, and left, head in the air, without saying goodbye. Coming from the same strong Methodist background as Mrs. Judd-Jones, whose mother, like my paternal grandmother, had been an active member of the WCTU— the Women's Christian Temperance Union—I knew I'd been too flip. I should have thought before I spoke.

However, relieved I now didn't have to offer the mandatory cup of tea and home-baked cookies, which I didn't have, I stoked the wood-stove and hurried to get dinner for Jim, who had an early evening meeting in Whitecourt. Several more phone calls came through, and in relaying the messages to Jim when he got home, I forgot all about the rum. We were just starting to eat when we saw the lights go on in the church basement. Bill Copeland, one of our two resident RCMP officers, was there, looking around in the kitchen. Jim said "Oh, he's probably picking up something his wife left at the last meeting of her young peoples' group."

Twenty minutes later, the officer phoned to tell us he had just picked up five bottles of rum from the church kitchen counter. Mrs. Judd-Jones had phoned and asked him to look into the matter. Did we have any idea where the bottles came from? We didn't, but suggested that some poor woman was in trouble with her husband for losing track of them. We couldn't imagine why she'd have them with her at the meeting, much less why she'd leave them in the church. Chuckling, Bill said, "As long as you don't drink it in the church, or bootleg it, you can store it there. But if no one claims it, it will have to go back to the Liquor Control Board in Edmonton tomorrow night. So would you try and find out who owns it?"

I said, "Perhaps I can make some judicious inquiries. If I find out who owns it, I'll call you."

Jim and I then tried to think which one of the Ladies' Aid members might have been taking home some rum, but we were stumped. Jim said, "You jolly well better be careful. Be sure you don't ask the wrong person." He then went off to his meeting in Whitecourt, and I spent the evening wondering how to be judicious. Finally I thought of Blanche Bentley, a former president of the Ladies' Aid who'd lived in town for some years and knew the other Aid members well enough to make a guess about the possible owner. I'd consulted her before on various other dilemmas and knew I could talk to her about this one. However, inquiries would have to wait until next day, because the Mayerthorpe phone exchange closed daily at four o'clock.

Blanche laughed when I told her and said, "I haven't the faintest idea whose rum would be."

"I'm sure it was left accidentally by someone who intended to take it home. She probably picked it up from one of her husband's cronies who brought it back from Edmonton." There followed a short horrified silence, which I could feel over the wires.

Finally Blanche said, "Uh-oh, you know, it's ours—well, not ours, but the Curling Club's. Tom picked it up for them when we were in Edmonton yesterday. It's for the two-bit bonspiel. The losers buy the winners a bottle. Whatever will Tom say when I tell him the RCMP have it?"

"Don't tell him," I said. "I'll phone the RCMP, and they'll probably bring it over and Tom won't know the difference."

But Tom had come in just then and overheard Blanche. He said, "What have the RCMP got that would matter to me?"

When she told him that Mrs. Judd-Jones had found some rum in the church basement and had called the RCMP, we all broke into hysterical laughter.

Tom said, "Good lord. Was it our rum? How on earth?"

"Well, it's a bit complicated," Blanche said. "The president of the Ladies' Aid called in here on her way to the meeting. She wanted to talk over some ideas she had about the spring tea and bake sale. Her arms were loaded down with bags of groceries she'd bought on the way, intending to take them home after the meeting. When we started off for the church, I offered to help her carry some of her bags. I hadn't got around to unwrapping the stuff we got in Edmonton, so I guess I must have picked up our bag with the rum, thinking it was one of hers. When she went home, she took her own bags and left mine. All those brown paper bags look the same. She probably could have told by the weight it wasn't hers. If she peeped inside, she might not have wanted to let on that she saw our rum. Cleaning up the kitchen after the Ladies' Aid had lunch, Mrs. Judd-Jones found the bag, and phoned the RCMP."

Long before noon, the story was all over town, assisted possibly by Mrs. George, who might have overheard my phone conversation with Blanche, and without mentioning any names reported that she'd heard rum was found in the church basement. I had an appointment that morning with the dentist. My mouth propped open, he said, "Well, I hear they're serving light refreshments in the church basement these days."

After Sunday service, the chair of the stewards came up to Jim and said with a twinkle, "I hear that since the manse was moved and now has no basement, the minister has to cache his liquor in the church." Then, more seriously, but smiling, he added, "A letter has already come in from one of our members, asking that you be strictly censured. She may ask for an investigation by Presbytery." Jim's response to this was, "Presbytery will sure have fun trying to censure my wife."

After the laughter died down, most people in the community were indignant that Mrs. Judd-Jones had called the RCMP. But Mrs. Judd-Jones said it was her duty to call. It was obvious that Mrs. Norquay, the United Church minister's wife, had not taken the matter seriously. Young ministers should be more careful about the kind of women they marry.

sixteen

You Need to Dress Up
for a Wedding

Saturday night was open house at the manse, when farmers and their wives, or sometimes only their wives, would drop in to talk about some problem they were having, or just to visit and wait until the rest of their family was ready to go home. We were never sure who would turn up, but we made a point of being home—which meant Jim made strenuous efforts to get his Sunday sermon in shape before the Saturday supper. One Saturday in the middle of the winter, George Fogan and his wife, Pauline, arrived from Karagana Hill.

They had been to a dance at Greencourt the week before, and when they left to go home they'd found thirteen-year-old Tommy Shingle shivering in the back of their truck. He said he was scared to go back to the Joe Muggridge farm, where he'd been placed, and begged to go home with them. Tommy had hitched a ride to Greencourt in the back of the truck of a neighbouring family who'd stopped at the Muggridges' to deliver some eggs on their way to the dance. They hadn't discovered him, and he didn't want to go home with them because they lived close to Muggridges and would be sure to take him back there. Joe Muggridge would beat him for running away and might make him sleep in the haymow, where he could freeze to death. The Fogans knew Joe Muggridge to be a hard man. They'd never trust *their* kids with him. The boy was obviously terrified to go back to the Muggridges, so the Fogans had taken him home with them.

During the couple of weeks Tommy lived with them, he gradually told them his story. He had been abandoned by his parents when he was two and had lived in an orphanage in Edmonton until the previous spring, when the provincial Department of Child Welfare had sent him to the Muggridges, it being a common practice to send orphans to farms where they could be put to work in return for room and board. Tommy said he couldn't do some of Joe's chores—he wasn't strong enough. He couldn't, for example, hoist a bale of straw onto the hay wagon once the load reached the second layer. He was supposed to make sure Mrs. Muggridge always had kindling for the cookstove, but he'd never been taught to use an axe. Joe hadn't shown him—he just told him if he kept on trying he'd teach himself. In the process, Tommy had cut a chunk out of one of his boots, barely missing his toes. Often, when Joe got really mad about something, he'd beat him and make him go without dinner.

The Fogans liked having Tommy. He was good company for Peter, who didn't have any friends his own age, and they were keen to have him stay. But had they done the wrong thing? Should they have asked permission from somebody? Would they get into trouble?

Jim said if he'd found the boy in his car, he'd have done the same thing. Had Joe told anyone Tommy was missing? George said Joe lived about seven miles down their road, but he hadn't come looking and probably didn't know Tommy was living with them. Pauline, George's wife, said, "It would be awful if Child Welfare sent him another boy to beat."

Jim said he didn't know what the regulations were, but he'd find out. He'd phone Child Welfare in Edmonton first thing Monday and let the Fogans know if there was a problem. Somewhat relieved, the Fogans went home.

The phone conversation with the Child Welfare department was instructive but shocking. Jim asked to speak to the minister, but could only get to someone who called himself an assistant to the minister. The assistant didn't seem at all concerned that Tommy had complained about being beaten or that he had run away from his placement or that Joe Muggridge had never reported Tommy missing. He merely said, "Well, what about the Fogan family? Are they a good family?"

Jim told him they were well-respected members of his Karagana Hill congregation. He was sure Tommy would not be ill treated in their home.

The response was, "Well, tell them to keep him." He didn't ask for the Fogans' full names or address. Nor did he ask Jim for his credentials. We were stunned to realize that the Child Welfare department kept no records of the children they placed on farms. Nor, apparently, did they check up on the quality, or the safety, of their placements.

We didn't know the Fogan family very well, because Karagana's Sunday service in the abandoned schoolhouse took place only once a month. Like other families, the Fogans turned up only when they could, when the roads were clear of snow or gumbo. Like other families in that area, they farmed on poor, wooded soil for a subsistence living. The chances were that they could barely support their own family, let alone another child. However the Fogans seemed very much on a par with other farm families we knew in the area, sharing a similar degree of poverty. So Jim reasoned that living with the Fogans was sure to be better than staying with Joe Muggridge. It was a month before the Fogans turned up again at the manse.

They had heard nothing from Muggridge. Tommy was still with them, and he enjoyed doing chores with Peter. But they had a problem. They'd never talked to anyone about it before and they needed advice. They told us that Peter, twelve years old, and Julie, fourteen, had both been deaf from birth and so hadn't learned to speak. Now that Tommy was living with them, playing and working with the children, he often got impatient when he couldn't make Peter and Julie understand what he was saying. They had become increasingly aware of how badly disadvantaged their children were going to be. Pauline, who before her marriage to George had been the teacher in the local one-room school, had managed somehow to teach both children to read and write in a limited way. But she had no idea how to teach them to speak. With farming the way it was, they thought Peter should learn a trade, but how could he go to school if he couldn't hear and couldn't speak? And if Julie couldn't hear or speak, she might never get a husband.

We had only recently heard about the Fogans' deaf children from one of their neighbours. They told us there was no cure and that George and his wife were extremely sensitive about it, treating it as something to be hidden. We had seen the family several times before and hadn't realized there was a problem. Like other farm kids, the Fogan children had been brought up to be seen and not heard. They *were* extremely shy, afraid to look at you. We were concerned about them but hadn't yet found a way to broach the subject of their deafness.

The Fogans told us that when Julie, their oldest, was born, she'd cried as loudly as other babies, but they finally became aware that she wasn't beginning to talk. She made various sounds that indicated what she wanted, but failed to say any real words. Then they realized she was deaf. When Peter came along, he had the same problem. Because the children couldn't hear, they hadn't learned to speak, and the Mayerthorpe doctor, with whom they had discussed it, had not suggested there was anything to be done. It hadn't occurred to them to seek any other advice. However, Tommy had told them that one of the bosses at his orphanage was deaf and had something stuck in his ear that allowed him to hear. Did we know of such a thing? Could we find out about it? Jim said he knew there were some inventions called hearing aids, which could often improve one's hearing. He'd look into it.

He thought his only recourse was to contact someone in Edmonton. He got in touch with Darrel Dunlop, who had been in his Peace River congregation but had moved to Edmonton. Darrel was a member of the Rotary Club, and through one of their members he was able to arrange appointments for Peter and Julie with specialists and to have them fitted with hearing aids. About six weeks later, when the Fogans got to Sunday service, George told us how excited Peter was when he'd heard milk going into the pail for the first time.

Pauline, greatly aided by Tommy, who delighted in helping, spent time each day working with the children on their speech, and she told us that, in the process, Tommy was improving his reading skills. As time passed, Peter and Julie began to acquire enough confidence to speak with people outside the family. Pauline got correspondence courses from the Department of Education and worked with all three children to get them ready for high school.

Some four years later, George turned up at the manse one afternoon when Jim was out to say that Peter had been accepted at a technical school in Edmonton and was being funded by the Rotary Club that had bought the hearing aids and had kept in touch with the family. Tommy, now seventeen, had a job pumping gas at Nelson's Garage in Mayerthorpe and hoped eventually to apprentice as a mechanic. I told George that I knew Jim would be delighted, and I asked him to stay for tea and tell me how Pauline and Julie were.

He said Julie was being married in a month's time and Pauline was going to great lengths to make the wedding a very special occasion. She had come in to Harrison's and used their Eaton's catalogue to order a wedding dress and veil for Julie and a "bride-mother's" dress for herself. The clothes hadn't come yet, but George was worried about the cost. Pauline was insisting that he buy a suit to wear. He'd never owned a suit, he wouldn't feel comfortable wearing one, and he knew he'd never wear it again. He couldn't afford it, but he didn't want to hurt Pauline.

So, he guessed, the only way he could hope to pay for all the new clothes was to sell his cow. They'd have to use canned milk like most everyone in town, but he wouldn't have to feed the children anymore, and with only Pauline and himself left in the house it might not matter much. He figured he'd better go to Harrison's and get out their catalogue and order the suit.

seventeen

Purged of Pity and Fear

After two weeks of twenty-below weather, I was suffering from cabin fever. So I called Hazel Stubbins, a woman who had produced some extraordinary costumes for a school Christmas pageant. No bathrobes. No bath towels. I said I was finding the cold depressing and was fed up with having frost on the inside of the front door every morning and having to keep restoking the furnace to keep from freezing. I thought we ought to do something to get us out of the house, something just for fun. "Why not organize a little theatre?"

Hazel said she didn't quite know what that was, but she always loved working on Christmas pageants. If I knew how to organize it, she'd be happy to help.

We did a lot of planning before we felt ready to call a meeting. We figured the only way to make it work was to get the three neighbouring villages along the highway to work together: our own village, Mayerthorpe, along with Sangudo, a few miles east, and Greencourt, a few miles west. The theatre would need a name and, to be acceptable, it would somehow have to recognize the participation of each village. With some discussion, we decided that we'd use the first letter in the name of each village, going from east to west. The SMG Little Theatre was hatched.

The next issue of the *Mayerthorpe Review* announced the place and date for the inaugural meeting and invited all those interested to attend. Hazel and I phoned people we knew in each village, and about twenty men and women turned up.

The plan was for each community to do a one-act play and then present all three plays on consecutive evenings in each village. Any equipment needed for lighting and sets would be owned and shared in common and paid for out of expected profits, which would be deposited in the Little Theatre bank account. Each village would be autonomous, appoint its own director, decide on the play, and cast the players. The

Little Theatre Board and executive would have representatives from each village. We asked the Extension Department of the University of Alberta to send us a bundle of one-act plays. Then, once we figured out who would do what, we were in business.

As president of the organization, I wrote to CFRN, a popular Edmonton radio station, and the local CBC affiliate to tell both about the project and request public-service announcements. CFRN responded with a letter that said they would make nine announcements, which would be equivalent to a donation of $78, and would ask Helen Kent to mention it on her women's program. CBC responded by asking Betty Thomlinson to feature the theatre on her show, as something new on the rural scene. Thomlinson said a community theatre organized by three rural villages along the Alaska Highway, with a combined population of under eight hundred, must be a first in Canada. The Mayerthorpe Chamber of Commerce, delighted by the publicity, heralded our initiative, and the cast members cherished the hope that someone might come out from Edmonton to report on it for the *Edmonton Journal*. Feeling nervously protective of our novice actors, I prayed no one would.

Because Mayerthorpe had the largest population and seating capacity, the first performance was held in our community hall. Our play was to come on right after Sangudo's production of *The Man in the Bowler Hat*, a play that seems to have disappeared utterly from the archives. The hall was a small frame building with a narrow stage but no wings or backstage where players could wait to go on. So we met to put on our costumes and makeup in Hazel Stubbins's living room, a five-minute walk down the road from the hall. We were doing Thornton Wilder's *Happy Journey*, a story about a family with two teenage children driving to see their married daughter, who'd just lost her newborn baby.

Hortense Buckam had got a book on stage makeup from the Extension lending library and considered herself an expert, an opinion not shared by all the actors. She worked slowly and methodically. If someone questioned her, she'd open her book to prove she was right. This slowed her down, and I began to worry that we wouldn't get ourselves together in time. Some of the actors kept disappearing into the room where they'd put their coats. They'd stay a few minutes and come back demanding to know when it would be their turn to be made up. Once, Hortense got delayed waiting for an actor who left her before she was quite finished with him. I couldn't figure it out.

I didn't catch on until Harold Stubbins, who was to play Pa, came out laughing uproariously with his arm around Rosemary, who was to play Ma. Then I got it. They were all going for a swig to buoy them up. That's why I'd been asked to hang my coat on the hook at the back of the front door. I didn't know what to do; obviously, they didn't want me to know. As a parson's wife from a strong Methodist tradition, I'd be expected to object. Not that I would have—at least not on religious grounds. They were all bundles of nerves, and I didn't want to upset them further. I decided to play dumb and pretend not to notice, though as time went on I occasionally got a whiff of beery breath. I just hoped it wouldn't get around that the parson's wife had condoned their drinking.

I looked at my watch and thought Sangudo would be about in the middle of their play. I was worried because it looked as if we might be late. Finally, we were all ready and out the door. However, Harold Stubbins, probably needing more fortification, said he'd forgotten his gloves and had to go back and get them. This took a surprising three or four minutes. By the time we finally set out, somewhat noisily, to walk the three or four blocks to the hall, Rosemary was complaining that the falling snow was ruining her makeup. When we got there, we weren't sure where they were in the program. There was only one entrance; players had to walk through the audience from the back to get to the stage. We didn't want to walk in on Sangudo's play, so we decided to wait outside till we heard the loud outburst of clapping that would signal the end of their play. It was twenty-five below, and snow was falling in large flakes. We stood huddled together, stamping our feet to keep warm, listening for clapping. We waited several minutes until Joey Baggs, who played Arthur and was wearing short pants, said his knees couldn't stand the cold any longer. He threw open the door and raced in, followed by the rest of us. The stage was empty. The whole audience turned around, clapping, cheering, whistling, catcalling.

We couldn't start right away, because the stage manager, who plays the role of narrator, had to put the car together and then set the scene for the audience. The car in Wilder's play is simulated with four chairs and a small platform that raises the back seat higher than the front, so the audience can see all the actors. We hadn't remembered to ask anyone to reserve the chairs we needed to make the car. All 150 chairs were being sat on, so we had to ask for volunteers from the audience to give up their seats. Rosemary's children offered theirs, Hortense's husband gave up his, and George Jensen from the hardware store, said, "You can sure have my seat. It's time I went home. Sangudo started late and who knows how long that fake car will take to get where it's going. I gotta go home and stoke my furnace. If I stay here much longer it will be out."

Finally the play began. The pace was pretty slow as the actor's fumbled for lines. They'd never have been arrested for going over the speed limit, though they might have been charged with driving under the influence. Pa kept mixing up his lines and Arthur, who forgot most of his, was brilliant at making them up. But no one knew how to pick up on what he said. Rosemary kept laughing hysterically all the way through. I was the prompter, but I couldn't figure out how to keep them on track. I sat on the bottom stair of the steps leading to the stage, out of direct view of the audience, so thankfully I could hide my embarrassment. However, I could see almost everybody who was there and was greatly relieved when I couldn't identify a CBC type or any *Edmonton Journal* reporter, not that I'd expected to see any.

As I sat there, I remembered that Aristotle said the purpose of drama was to purge the emotions of pity and fear. I didn't think our production would quite do that.

eighteen

Too Bad They Don't
Brew Beer

The day after the inaugural performance of the SMG Little Theatre, old Mr. Torgenson celebrated his eighty-fifth birthday. He was a retired farmer who had lived in the community for many years, and was known for miles around for his storytelling about the old days when the first settlers arrived. The notice in the *Mayerthorpe Review* had invited the whole community to come by at any time between two and six. I didn't know Mr. Torgenson myself, but I knew his daughter Laura quite well, and thought I should pay my respects to her father, one of Mayerthorpe's earliest pioneers—especially as Jim was unable to come on that day. I also looked forward to connecting with the broader community at a gathering where I'd likely meet people I'd never see at church.

A few minutes after four that afternoon, I arrived at the door of Mr. Torgenson's small house. I could see through the window that the room was crowded and the guests were having a good time, talking and laughing and drinking beer. Mr. Torgenson was clearly enjoying himself, encircled by a group of local farmers who looked to be listening avidly to one of his stories. When I walked in, the talking and laughter ceased instantly. Everyone got up and said they really had to leave. They wanted to get home before dark, or they had to pick up something at the Co-op before it closed. In minutes, the room emptied. Mr. Torgenson looked stunned. Laura asked if I wouldn't sit down and have a cup of tea.

I was mortified. I had obviously spoiled Mr. Torgenson's party. Why hadn't I known they'd all be drinking beer and feel uncomfortable in the presence of the minister's wife? Why hadn't I realized beforehand that they'd expect my disapproval and be embarrassed? When would I learn? Why hadn't I suggested that Jim and I go together to see Mr. Torgenson the next day or the day before the party? I felt sick. But now I had to stay for tea and try to salvage the situation.

I extended greetings from Jim and explained that he had planned to come to the party but couldn't, as he had to conduct a funeral down country and wouldn't be home until after supper. At this Mr. Torgenson brightened slightly and said, "In the old days when someone died, we had ne'er a church or a parson, or Charlie Bromely's hearse. Old Mrs. Richardson always volunteered to lay out the corpse, bathe it, and get it dressed for burial. My neighbour, the next concession down, always made the casket with timber cut from his bushlot. Friends of the departed would dig the grave, and gather round while the coffin was lowered. A person can't be decently buried unless we calls on his Maker; so I always read the Lord's Prayer for 'em. That's all I knew to do." That got Mr. Torgenson started, and he went on to tell me about some of his hunting expeditions.

"In the early days, if we hadn't wild game to eat, we'd have starved. So we hunted moose, deer, and sometimes elk. All you can hunt now is rabbits and prairie chickens." After several other stories, one concerning an attack by a bear, I thanked him for the tea and stories and left for home. But I knew I hadn't made up for the sudden loss of all his other guests.

Until I'd left the house, the manse phone had rung constantly all that day with accolades for the SMG's performance the night before. Players and audiences from all three villages were ecstatic, and wanted to know when we would do it again. The enthusiasm was such that I felt chagrined: I had viewed the quality of the performance with such dismay and wondered what I had been thinking. Most of the players had never been in a play before. None had ever seen a professional production and few even a good amateur one. The response from strangers all over the district had made me feel I might finally be accepted as an ordinary citizen like anyone else and not continue to be thought of as a "holier-than-thou parson's wife." But Mr. Torgenson's party had fractured that hope.

A couple of weeks later the SMG executive met and made plans to mount another production in late spring, with three different one-act plays. Plays were decided on, casts selected, and the whole process started over. Basking in the glow of the enthusiastic reception of our first production, our meeting to plan the next show was jubilant. We planned to open in Sangudo on April 18.

The night of April 17 there was a terrible snowstorm. It lasted for two days, closing all the roads and decimating the audiences for both Sangudo and Mayerthorpe. We worried that our proceeds would fail to meet expenses but hoped to sell out in Greencourt for our last performance, despite that many roads might still be impassable.

The Mayerthorpe group was doing J. M. Barrie's *The Old Lady Shows Her Medals*, a play in which an old Scottish washerwoman invents a son and finds to her surprise that a fine, upstanding soldier adopts her as his mother. We were last on the program, so we planned to put on makeup and costumes in the two-room schoolhouse beside the small hall where the plays were to be presented. We set out with six of us in the car, the four women who played the old ladies, myself, and Harold Stubbins, who'd agreed to drive us. Bill Copeland, our local RCMP officer who was playing the minister, was bringing Joey Baggs, who would play the soldier.

We were about five miles out of Mayerthorpe when Rosemary announced that she had forgotten the tin of oysters that were to dub for winkles during the tea-party scene. They wouldn't take my advice and fake them but insisted we detour eight miles to Blue Ridge, where there was a variety store that stayed open in the evenings. Harold Stubbins, who was not in the play, was the most insistent that we detour. At Blue Ridge, three of us got out of the car; Rosemary to go to the store, I to stretch my legs from sitting four in the back seat, and Harold, who made straight for the men's entrance to the hotel pub. Still feeling the sting of spoiling Mr. Jorgenson's birthday party, and wanting Harold to know there was no way I would play the moral police, I followed him closely, only a couple of feet behind. We were almost at the door when Harold turned and said in a shaky voice, "Mrs. Norquay, you can't come in here."

"Okay, Harold, but when we get back to town, I'll tell everyone you asked me for a date and then stood me up."

"You wouldn't."

"I just might." And with that I returned to the car. But I was a bit worried. Was he going for a drink or just to the john? Men did all the driving in that country. None of us women had a licence. I had no idea what, if anything, I could or should do.

Rosemary was already back in the car. We waited for well over half an hour, getting colder by the minute. Finally, Harold arrived with a slight whiff of beer about him and a full case in hand. In no time five bottles were opened and we started off. Harold held his beer in one hand and steered the car with the other. He soon got well beyond the speed limit, but otherwise his driving seemed all right. I hoped it would stay that way for the twenty or so minutes we would need to reach

Greencourt. We'd probably make it unless we hit a patch of ice. I felt tense, but at the same time I inwardly chuckled at what Mrs. Judd-Jones would say if she heard that the minister's wife had driven in a car full of drinking passengers and a drinking driver. Then with a jolt I realized, that unlike Torgenson's guests, *this* group wasn't inhibited by the minister's wife. This felt good—but would there be repercussions if the news got back to town?

When we arrived at Greencourt, the second play was not quite finished. The whole show had started late to allow its audience time to arrive through snowdrifts on unploughed sideroads. I was relieved to see the RCMP car parked outside the schoolhouse, which meant the minister and soldier had managed to get there. We figured we had just enough time to put on our makeup and costumes.

Our play had not gone very well at either Mayerthorpe or Sangudo. But in this production, the actors threw themselves into it in a way they had never done before, and they clearly moved the audience, some of whom later confessed to tears. Greencourt had planned a dance after the performance, on the theory that no one in *their* community would buy a ticket just for a play. Given the lateness of the hour, we decided not to stay for the dance; it had started snowing again and visibility was rapidly diminishing. Bill Copeland suggested that we travel home in a convoy in case of difficulties. I thought that was great. With the RCMP following us, Harold wouldn't risk drinking, and we'd drive at a more decorous speed.

Flushed with feelings of success, the talk going home was animated. Rosemary had heard from a cousin in Red Deer about the annual one-act-play festival held by the Alberta Drama League. She thought we should enter a play next year. If we won, we might get to play in the Dominion Drama Festival. The talk then shifted to a discussion of what play to present and who should be in it. Harold dropped us off one by one and got home with his case of beer, minus five bottles.

Ten days later, on a cold wintry afternoon, I walked to the post office and found two letters in our box, both addressed to the SMG president. I hurried home and sat down in the warm kitchen to read them. The first letter was from Sangudo, from Bill and Emily Smithers, the young couple who co-chaired the local group and had built the sets for our first production. They felt they would have to resign unless some basic ground rules could be established to insure fairness in decisions about play selection, casting, and division of responsibilities. They had been left with all the preparatory work for the second production because the older members of the community had frozen out the younger ones, who had started out with great enthusiasm. Old Mr. Fraggins had rounded up a bunch of his friends and had managed to swing the vote to *The Monkey's Paw*, a play none of the others wanted but one in which Fraggins saw himself in the lead role. In addition, Fraggins had insisted that Emily direct the play but then refused to take any direction.

The second letter came from Greencourt, enclosing three bills: the first to cover the cost of extending their stage, which they had deemed too small, the second for new lighting equipment, which they assured me each group could use in turn, and the third to pay the orchestra for the dance they'd held after the show. They weren't sending us the ticket proceeds from the play because the lead actors had refused to perform unless the money went to the Red Cross. They were sending all the bills to me because our secretary-treasurer, who was the principal of the two-room school, had resigned.

Next day I got a phone call from the county school superintendent, the SMG vice-president who lived in Sangudo. He'd heard about our difficulties and blamed himself for not sitting in often enough on Sangudo's planning meetings; he'd left them to function entirely on their own. He would call them all together and try to set down some guidelines. There was another teacher in Greencourt who, he thought, would do a better job than the secretary-treasurer who'd resigned— a man, who would take some responsibility for pulling that group together. He thought once everybody calmed down, they would undoubtedly vote to continue at the next general meeting.

Rosemary's cousin must have had something to do with the letter I received a few days later. To my amazement, it came from the president of the Dominion Drama Festival. He said that spring marked the beginning of the fourth year of the partnership between the DDF and Calvert Distillers Ltd.: *The company has rescued the organization from folding by its generous sponsorship, and starting this month, there will be Calvert advertisements in newspapers and magazines across Canada, emphasizing Canadian theatre and the Dominion Drama Festival. Each and every friend of DDF—and their friends, when the occasion arises— can remember and support Calvert's* [whisky]. *Increased Calvert sales mean increased Calvert budgets for DDF.*

Well, I thought, too bad they don't brew beer.

nineteen

Scrub Trees May
Have Deep Roots

It was summer, and I was at Surprise Lake Camp with our two younger children. I had just assured the chore boys that we now had enough wood to keep the kiln firing all night when we heard a car coming down the camp road. In a few minutes Slim Collins appeared through the trees. "Marg, the RCMP have been looking for you all day. Jim's had an accident and you are to phone your brother in Cooksville. I've come to take you to Edson so you can phone him."

Alarmed, I ran to our cabin, picked up a sweater, and told our babysitter, Maggie, that Jim had been involved in some kind of an accident. I was off to Edson to phone home and would be back in an hour. I would tell the camp mother, on my way out, so she would take charge while I was away. By now, the chore boys would have told everyone else.

As far as I knew, Jim was on Manitoulin Island, which had been devastated by a hurricane, helping his brother Eddie clear up around the family cottage. He'd taken four-year-old Sara with him to visit Grandmother Norquay, who she hadn't seen Sara since she was a baby. When I contacted my brother Rob, he said Eddie had phoned from Sudbury to say Jim had been injured falling out of a tree, but he didn't think it was serious. But he thought I should phone Jim's mother for details the next morning, it being too late to phone her that night.

I returned to camp, not particularly worried. The trees on that part of the island were all short and stunted, so Jim couldn't have fallen far. He probably had a few bruises and was a bit shaken up. When I got back to Surprise Lake, the whole camp had stayed up, anxious to find out what had happened. When I told them it wasn't serious, that Jim had just fallen out of a small scrub tree, they were so relieved they almost laughed. Only the week before, they'd seen him precariously perched on top of the craft house, trying to mend the roof. One of the staff offered to drive me to Edson next morning right after breakfast to phone Jim's mother. Calmly, we all went to bed.

After breakfast, the counsellors and campers headed off to the kiln to find out how their clay pots had come through the firing. Since the kiln was just off the parking lot, I walked along with them, and couldn't resist stopping briefly to watch as they opened the kiln, which was emptied in minutes. There were the usual cries of delight when a piece came out whole, and groans of disappointment when someone's pot had fallen apart. The campers then went off to do breakfast dishes and clean up their cabin, and I walked to the parking lot. I was surprised to see a car on the camp road, coming toward us from the highway. It stopped, and its driver, Darrel Dugan, a young man in our Edmonton congregation, told us he'd heard about Jim's accident and knew I'd want to get home. I never thought of asking him how he had heard about it, or even what he had heard. Camp was closing the next day and, given the accident, however slight, I thought Jim might not make it back to pick us up as soon as we'd planned. Going home with Darrel seemed like such a good idea that I completely forgot about phoning Jim's mother. Leaving senior camp staff in charge, we piled into the car: two-year-old Robbie, seven-month-old Naomi, Maggie, and I, together with playpen, carriage, diaper pail, and a few toys.

When we got home to the manse, the whole street came out to greet us, bringing casseroles of food, offers to put the children to bed, and all kinds of advice, and telling me to be sure to take a sleeping pill so I'd get a good night's sleep. I was completely mystified, turned down all offers of help, put the children to bed myself, followed them without a sleeping pill, and planned to phone the next morning as instructed—not realizing the "next morning" had already gone. I've never been able to figure out why I didn't phone as soon as I got home that day. I must have been in shock, brought on by the contagion of community concern.

In the morning, I phoned Jim's mother. She said Jim was much better that day than he had been the day before. She didn't sound worried; she said Jim had never lost consciousness, but gave no further details except to say that Eddie had driven Jim to the hospital in Little Current to get his cuts attended to, and the doctors there arranged for him to be flown to Sudbury General. By this time I was totally alarmed, not only about Jim, but also about four-year-old Sara, who must be stricken, wondering where her Daddy had gone and in the care of a grandmother she didn't know.

Not satisfied with what Jim's mother had told me, I phoned my own mother, in Cooksville, and asked her to find out what had happened. I knew she would go immediately to Sudbury, march into the hospital, tell them she was a 1915 graduate of Toronto General, and insist on knowing the condition of her son-in-law. She'd also take care of Sara, who might feel relatively secure with this grandmother, because Mother had visited us several times and Sara and I had stayed with my parents for three months in Cooksville when I'd had to vacate the Mayerthorpe manse while a new foundation was put in. When I finished talking to Mother, I realized it would take her at least another day to get to Sudbury. Now, frantic to know more, I phoned our Edmonton family doctor, known to my children as Uncle Henry, and asked him to phone the hospital in Sudbury to find out what had happened.

Uncle Henry got back to me within a couple of hours. He said the article in the *Edmonton Journal* that all my neighbours had read had got it right—Jim's skull was fractured in three places. He had been kneeling on the trunk of a partly uprooted tree, sawing off branches, when suddenly the tree snapped upright, throwing him onto sandstone rocks in two feet of water at the edge of the lake. The Sudbury hospital hadn't the capacity to deal with such an injury and planned to send him by train to Toronto General. I should make immediate plans to go to Toronto. By this time, Robbie and Naomi had picked up on my tension and were constantly wailing. I was traumatized. Within a couple of hours, a family friend turned up and gently asked if I had made my train reservation. I hadn't. Another friend helped me get packed, thoughtfully putting in winter clothes for all three children, something I hadn't thought of, and in a couple of days we were on our way.

Sara was with my parents when they met us at the station, and I can still see her running joyfully down the platform, delighted to see us. Jim had arrived at Toronto General by then, and I planned to see him the next day before I spoke to the surgeon. When finally I did see Jim, he looked like someone I'd never seen before. All his hair was shaved off, and he had a gash that went from the top of his head across his forehead and face, ending at the bottom of his nose. He didn't seem surprised to see me. His opening words were, inexplicably, "Make sure you get enough rest." That had been his parting advice when he took us to the camp, just before he left for Manitoulin Island. When I asked if he was in any pain, he said he wasn't and hadn't been. He wasn't quite sure what had happened, but expected to get up soon. He had to get back to the church.

The surgeon confirmed the skull fractures. It was not a case of life or death; Jim would live, but he wasn't sure what quality of life he would have. He would operate the next day and then meet with me a couple of days later. I went home to my parents and my children feeling quite numb, not daring to wonder what kind of a life Jim and our family were about to face. In a desperate effort to persuade myself that normal life would go on, I played more singing games than usual before I put the children to bed: *There was a princess long ago, long ago ... I'm a little teapot short and stout ... Eentsy-weentsy spider.*

Two days later, the operation completed, I went to see the surgeon. He said Jim's brain had not been lacerated, as he expected, but only bruised. Jim would recover. He would have to stay in hospital another four or five days until the incisions healed, but full recovery would take some months.

During that time, we stayed in my parents' downstairs apartment, which my father had built in case any of his grown children might need, for some reason, to return home. Jim took some time to realize he was not in any shape to return to Edmonton and kept saying he had to get home and get back to work. I had to intercept more than one letter he wrote to the church Board telling them he'd be back the next week. The surgeon told him he could go back only after he had written two sermons he wouldn't be ashamed to preach. Jim thought he could do it in a couple of weeks, but his energy level was so low that it took him several months.

Meanwhile, we were fortunate in the enormous amount of support we were given from all sides. Public health care had not yet been invented, but doctors were never known to send a bill to ministers, so no bill arrived from the surgeon. I now realize that I never saw a bill from the hospital either, so I expect my parents intercepted it and paid for it. We also got enormous support from our congregation, who continued to pay Jim's salary, organized a drive for funds, and sent an additional cheque for several hundred dollars. Every day when I went to the post box, there were letters from friends, from current and former members of Jim's various congregations, from Edmonton, Mayerthorpe, Peace River, and from his student mission fields in rural

Saskatchewan. All wished him well, telling him they were praying for him, that they looked forward to seeing him back on his feet. I've always felt it was these daily messages and prayers that restored him to health. Finally, after about six months, Jim had his two sermons written and we were ready to go home.

The doctor gave me only three pieces of information and advice before we left: Jim should take it easy at first, but going back to work was essential to his full recovery; he might suffer a kind of emotional flatness for some time; and he was not to drive the car for another three months. But we had no idea of the fallout that would come from the story in the *Edmonton Journal*.

twenty

Sympathy and Prejudice Come
with a Crack on the Head

When we got off the train at Edmonton, we were welcomed by several members of the congregation and escorted home to find a refrigerator full of homemade casseroles, bread, milk, and fresh vegetables. The chairman of the Board arrived within half an hour to tell Jim they'd arranged for someone to assist him conducting Sunday services. All he had to do was preach the sermon. He was to take it easy and not work too hard.

The children appeared to be delighted to be home again sleeping in their own rooms, but that first night I had to get up three times, as one after the other woke up crying and took considerable soothing before going back to sleep. They had never done this while at their grandparents' house, so I assumed they had picked up some tension from their father or me that I wasn't aware of.

The next day we got up and had breakfast about eight, and Jim hurried off to the church, anxious to get back to work. After a couple of days, the children settled down, and life went on pretty much as it had before the accident. About a week after we'd arrived home, when the children were having their afternoon nap, I was visited by two Edmonton ministers, each from one of the two large downtown churches. They got to the point immediately.

They thought Jim should not attempt to continue his ministry, and that he should resign as soon as possible. Shaken, but determined to sound calm, I replied that the surgeon had said going back to work was essential to his full recovery. Why did they think he should leave? Well, they thought being a minister, especially in a church that was just getting started in a new housing area, would be too difficult for a man who had had a head injury. I said that both the surgeon and our family doctor thought Jim could handle the work, and that he had been looking forward to coming back. Did they know of anyone else who thought Jim should resign? With some hums and haws, they finally said that a Dr. Harms, a church member, had come to see them and told them he'd been in touch with several people and the whole congregation was uneasy and wanted Jim to leave. I said, considering the warmth with which we had been greeted, I found that rather curious, but I would go and speak with Dr. Harms. With that, they left.

I didn't know much about Dr. Harms except that he'd been an enthusiastic fundraiser in the Wells campaign to raise money to pay the mortgage on our new church, which had allowed the congregation to move out of rumpus rooms and school gymnasiums. Living in a new housing development rapidly filling up with young families, Dr. Harms had, a year previously, demanded that Jim immediately visit anyone who moved into the area to urge them to join our church. Jim had said his first responsibility was to look after the congregation he already had—some 250 families with about 500 children. He would welcome any new arrivals who turned up at church but didn't have time to go prospecting. I remembered Jim saying that Dr. Harms had not been pleased with his response.

What to do? I couldn't tell Jim about the visit of his ministerial brethren, at least not until I'd investigated what they'd told me. As a lawyer's daughter, I knew I shouldn't go to see Dr. Harms without a witness, so I called George Lamb, a member of the Board whom I knew I could trust. He was shocked at my message and readily agreed to go with me to see Dr. Harms.

Our conversation with Dr. Harms was brief. He said that his goal was to enlarge the congregation as fast as possible. He wanted a man who would work ten hours a day, seven days a week, for the church. Obviously with his injury, Jim couldn't do that. Dr. Harms hadn't discussed the matter with the Board, but he was sure most people felt as he did. I should advise Jim to resign. I said I couldn't make such a promise, and with that we left. That night, each child, one after the other, woke up crying.

First thing next morning, after Jim had gone to the church, there was a phone message from old Mr. Torgenson in Mayerthorpe, asking Jim to visit his daughter Laura, who was dying of cancer in the Royal Alexandra Hospital. She had told her father that despite the terrible pain, she couldn't die until Jim was back to bury her. I phoned Jim at the church, and he said he would go immediately to see Laura. Then I phoned Uncle Henry, our family doctor, and told him some people thought Jim should resign. He said that at this point in Jim's recovery, resignation could have serious consequences. If in the end Jim had to step down, I should try to put off the news of it as long as possible. He saw no reason why Jim couldn't do the job. It was just ignorant prejudice to think he couldn't.

The next thing was to find out whether Dr. Harms's assessment of the will of the congregation was accurate. Since I knew Jim was greatly loved by a sizeable number of people, such an interpretation would have to be done by some outside objective authority. I knew Jim wouldn't under any circumstances stay where he wasn't wanted and would never want to do anything that created a rift in the congregation. If the congregation wanted him to leave, he would go without fuss. So I called the chair of the Edmonton Presbytery, the body assigned to support and advise United Church congregations and, if need be, to intervene. Given the information, the chair said he would take it from there.

I knew it would take some time for the Presbytery to get a committee together, to meet with the church Board and probably with the whole congregation. I was filled with tension and worry, but we went on with life more or less normally for several weeks. I felt guilty not telling Jim anything about the issue. We continued to have three children wake up crying every night. In the past, Jim and I had taken turns getting up with the children, and Jim was often the first to wake to the sound of a crying child. But since the accident, Jim never responded. The surgeon had told me that the bruises on Jim's brain would make him emotionally flat for some time, so I thought perhaps that was why a child's cry never woke him up. Ever since he left the hospital, we all witnessed this emotional flatness in his response to any sign of a need for affection or comfort, from either myself or the children, who continued to be unsettled. I felt entirely on my own. Sara, by this time nearly five, must have somehow overheard some adult discussion, because one day she asked, "Mommy, why don't some people like my Daddy?" Stunned, I said lamely, "I don't think anyone dislikes your Daddy," and quickly changed the subject. The question quite disturbed me. What had she heard and from whom?

Getting up for three crying children every night, trying to carry on life as usual with a secret I couldn't tell Jim, and waiting to hear from the Presbytery committee about our fate took a considerable toll. There was no one I dared discuss it with. I'd get up bleary-eyed in the morning and found getting breakfast a struggle. More than once, I'd intend to put a jug of milk on the table and miss the table altogether. I'd wash the breakfast dishes praying for strength.

Meanwhile, I was beginning to learn the depth of the common public consensus that anyone with a head injury would not be able to function normally and was quite possibly insane. Old Mr. Torgenson's daughter had died just hours after Jim visited her, and a friend told me about meeting someone who said she'd heard Jim had conducted a funeral. She was sure it couldn't be true. How could he have done it? Some of the clergy were as bad as the general public. It got so I hated to go with Jim to gatherings of United Church people outside our congregation. Almost every minister in the crowd would come up to me and say in a hushed voice, as if my answer would be something to be covered up, "And how is Jim?"

Finally, we got word that Dr. Harms had been acting only on his own initiative and that the congregation clearly wanted Jim to stay on. By the end of April, Jim's mental faculties had improved to the point that he began to plan the high school work camp and to recruit volunteer cabin leaders, and he was looking forward to another building project for Surprise Lake. But it was a good two years before he heard a child cry in the night.

twenty-one

Recycling Gallon Cans

Three years after we moved to suburban Edmonton, I was directing the camp for the eight-to-ten-year-olds at Surprise Lake while Jim was away on a week's study leave. I had just finished putting my three children to bed with the help of Maggie Schmit, our faithful young babysitter, when our camp cook appeared at the cabin door, quietly beckoning me to come out. Cookie drew me away toward the wash house, where we knew no one would be until bedtime, if then. She said in a low voice that she thought we had a bear. After the campers had finished the dishes and she'd cleaned up the kitchen, she'd gone back to her cabin and noticed that the compost heap had been disturbed. The peelings from the last two days had disappeared, and she was sure the two saucer-like indentations in the mud were made by bear paws. It was unusual for bears to venture this far south, but the forest fires raging up north that year may well have driven them from their usual habitat. She thought there was nothing to worry about in the daytime, because bears don't like noise, but we'd need to be careful going to the biffies at night. She would help round up the staff so we could figure out what to do. The only person not available at the moment was the swimming instructor, who was supervising a volleyball game. But all the rest would be free to come.

Most of the counselling staff that year were young couples from our Edmonton congregation, happy to volunteer their vacation time because they could bring their whole family and have an inexpensive holiday. Most of their children would be campers. Preschool children slept in the camper cabins with one of their parents and were looked after during the day in the tot lot, staffed by teenagers we'd trained to be babysitters. The young fathers were all returned veterans, just beginning their careers.

When we got the staff together, our first concern was how to keep the children from leaving their cabins to go to the biffy without alarming them about the bear. The camp mother said we had one or two occasional bedwetters and she hoped not to have any more occasions. We only had a few unused mattress ticks left and barely enough straw to fill them. The cook said she'd kept most of the empty gallon cans that our fruit and vegetables came in, and we could give each cabin at least two to use in the night. The nurse said she'd heard on her battery radio that the weather was expected to get dramatically colder in the next few days. It was already colder than it had been at the same time the night before. We could tell the campers that tonight they were to use the cans because we didn't want them to get cold running out to the biffies in their pyjamas. The camp mother and the nurse said they would distribute the cans while the children were still out on the playing field. We could tell them at campfire that we didn't want anyone going out to a biffy that night. The rest of us could figure out what to do about the bear.

Dave Glaxton, who was minding a cabin of eight-year-old boys, started off the discussion. "It's okay for tonight, but what about tomorrow night? What if a bear does turn up in the daytime? I'll go to town right now and buy a shotgun. I was in the infantry during the war and was top of my unit in target practice. I know how to handle a gun. A bear wouldn't be any problem."

Darrel Dugan jumped in and said, "I was a rear gunner in the air force. I'd love to take on shooting a bear. If Dave's going to town, I'd like to go with him."

Darrel's wife said she knew her ten-year-old girls would be scared if they knew there was a bear in the camp, but she herself would be more scared if she knew someone was walking around camp with a gun. "I'm a long-time member of the Society for the Prevention of Cruelty to Animals," she said, "and I'm really against shooting a bear or any other wild animal."

George Jessup said if Dave was driving to Edson he'd like to go too. He'd only worked for the quartermaster stores when he was in the army, but he was a bit of an authority on guns because his father had been a gun collector. He could give good advice on what to buy. Dave, anxious to drive to Edson as soon as possible, said he thought Darrel and George should go with him, find the gun shop and buy a gun. But the women said, almost with one voice, that none of the men should go to Edson. They didn't want to be left alone with all the boys, their own cabins of girls, and possibly a bear.

I knew we could easily *borrow* a gun in Edson, but I didn't want a bunch of novice hunters running around camp with a firearm. So I said I didn't know of any place in Edson where you could buy a gun, and anyway all the shops would now be closed. I told them Slim Collins would be bringing out supplies from Edson right after breakfast, and I'd get some advice from him. We'd have to go with the gallon cans for that night, and tomorrow we would figure out what to do. We'd cancel all the wilderness hikes and overnights until the problem was solved. It was now time for campfire, so the discussion was over.

The night passed without incident, and in the morning, much to my relief, Slim Collins turned up as expected. When I met with him and Cookie to tell him what supplies we'd need for the next week, we told him about the bear. He said he wasn't surprised. A bear had been seen in the bushlot of a nearby farm, and he'd brought us his shotgun so we could defend ourselves.

"For goodness' sake, Slim," I said, "don't tell anybody, and don't let anyone see it. I don't want any of our staff running around with a gun. I'm sorry, but you'll have to take it back."

Almost offended, Slim wanted to know why. "All the men are vets. They'd be relieved to have a gun on the premises. If they got the bear, they'd be able to brag to their pals back home how they had defended helpless woman and children. Where else can a red-blooded Canadian male get to do that anymore?"

I said that shooting a bear mightn't be as easy as shooting a man, and insisted he had to take the gun back. However, I asked him whether we couldn't have someone come out from the Hinton Forestry office. "Aren't they supposed to look after stray bears?"

"I guess they are," he said. "I'll phone Forestry when I got back to Edson."

Banking on such a possibility, I called a staff meeting at rest hour and said I thought the Forestry office would send a ranger to deal with the bear but that we'd have to use the gallon cans for another night. Darrel said that didn't matter to him. His boys used the bushes by the cabin. I didn't ask what happened in the other boys' cabins but I could see the women, still apprehensive about the bear, would be happy to use the gallon cans again. I could feel the men's disapproval of me for not having allowed them to deal with the bear in their own way. Dave demanded to know whether the forest ranger was coming for sure. I could only say I knew Slim would get in touch with the

Forestry office, which was responsible for looking after stray bears. It was already getting colder, so our ostensible reason for not letting the campers leave the cabins at night would still seem sound. Laura Dugan wanted to know what the forest ranger would do, as she was strongly opposed to shooting the bear. Surely it could be trapped. I could only say that we'd have to leave that to the forest ranger.

I hoped and prayed the ranger would come. I thought we'd have another visit from Slim if the ranger couldn't make it, but without a phone I couldn't find out for sure. I was on pins and needles all day, with one staff member after another anxiously asking if I'd heard back from Slim Collins. It was a long day, but the ranger arrived just after the campers had had their nightly hot cocoa and were back in their cabins getting ready for the night.

The ranger said there was no way to return the bear to his natural habitat. Once a bear tastes human food and finds it easy to get, it continues to be a nuisance and a threat if disturbed. The only thing to do was to shoot it. By morning he'd probably have it shot and buried. He'd hide overnight in the wash house, which would provide some protection from the weather. The wash house walls were only shoulder height, so the compost heap would be in full view.

I retired to our cabin, where I thankfully found my children and Maggie sound asleep. I went to bed with my clothes on but stayed awake all night. About five in the morning, I heard a shot, leapt out of bed, and ran to the kitchen, where Cookie was making an early breakfast for the ranger. He came in about ten minutes later to tell us he'd shot the bear but hadn't killed it, and the bear had stumbled off. The ranger said he'd have some breakfast and after an hour go out again to find the bear. By then the animal would have weakened enough through loss of blood to be approached safely. It was a long hour, in which I learned more about bears than I could have imagined there was to know. Finally the ranger left us, saying that when he got the bear he'd simply bury it and leave camp.

Fifteen minutes later we heard another shot. When the campers came for breakfast, a couple of the boys who lived on farms said they thought they'd heard gunshots in the night. "Someone must have been shooting coons."

While the campers washed the dishes and tidied up their cabins, the staff met briefly to review the night's events. Allison Davie's counsellor reported that no one in her cabin had needed to go out in the night, but Allison, having drunk two extra cups of cocoa, had to get up about four o'clock. The counsellor helped Allison find a gallon can in the dark, but she refused to use the can because it was full of tadpoles she was planning to take home. In their attempt to find the other can, they knocked it over. This can had been filled with Susy Smither's tadpoles, but at least now Allison had an empty one to use. Susy was tearful all through breakfast because all *her* tadpoles had died. She couldn't go and get more because she couldn't use a dirty can.

Dave Claxton said, "For heaven's sakes, there's lots more tadpoles. She can have one of our cans—two, if she wants, because we never used them. What I want to know is where the bear is buried. I want to go and mark the spot. Next year when I come back to camp, I'll dig it up and take out the skull. It will make a great trophy to show my friends."

"Well," said George Jessop, "you might at least lend it to me once in a while, so I could show *my* friends."

Darrel added, "My wife wouldn't have a trophy like that in our house, but you might let me have a couple of his teeth. I could put them on my key chain."

"Well," I said, "that's one way of getting staff for next year."

twenty-two

Founding Edmonton's United Community Fund

In 1956, Doris Anderson's *Chatelaine* was almost required reading for middle-class women. These were the mothers of the baby-boom generation and, hemmed in with small children, they often yearned for intellectual stimulation. Jim had just been appointed the minister of a church in a new suburb on the western edge of Edmonton. His congregation consisted almost entirely of young families. The fathers were veterans returned from the Second World War, and the women, many with advanced education, were stay-at-home mothers.

Within a month of settling in the manse, I got a phone call from the Women's Association, no longer dubbed the Ladies' Aid, asking me to come to their meeting and tell them about child welfare services in Alberta. They said they became concerned by an article in *Chatelaine* about religious barriers to adoption in Ontario, barriers that created a serious lack of adoptive homes. What was the situation in Alberta? they wondered.

Some of their mothers had been members of the Imperial Order of the Daughters of the Empire when it sponsored the Charlotte Whitton report, which exposed serious problems with Alberta's Child Welfare department. The report was swept under the rug by government authorities, and these young women suspected not much had changed, hence their request for information. Our experience in Mayerthorpe with the Fogan family and the provincial Child Welfare department over farm placements of orphans had indicated serious problems, but apart from that I knew nothing of substance. I phoned the Edmonton Information Service, which found a social worker who had worked for the department and was now a stay-at-home mother herself. She was prepared to come and speak to us about Alberta's Child Welfare, with the proviso that we not name or quote her in our minutes as the source of the information. The result of her talk was that we decided to organize a study group on Child Welfare, seek additional information, and try to affect some changes.

Over the next couple of years we tackled a number of social concerns: the lack of required standards in home-based private daycare, the need for professionally trained social workers in the welfare department, and the problem of newspapers' reporting fatal accidents in the oil fields before family members had been notified (this was a common practice at the time).

By our fourth year, a great deal of public dissatisfaction had grown around the functioning of the Community Chest, a precursor to the modern United Way. So when a group of local businessmen called a public meeting to organize a United Community Fund to replace the Chest, our study group decided to attend. By this time we were knowledgeable about many community services, some of which we considered inadequate. We decided to attend the meeting, and the group asked me to be their spokesperson.

The meeting was held in the high school auditorium, at the time the hall with the largest seating capacity. The entire power structure of the city was there on the stage: the mayor, the chair of the Chamber of Commerce, the chair of the Labour Council, the Community Services Council, a couple of MPPs, two prominent local CEOs, a retired brigadier general, and Edmonton's archbishop. The meeting began with laudatory introductions of all those on stage, followed by a number of speeches, almost all of which castigated the Community Chest for failing to live up to its goals. Then came the presentation of a slate of officers to be elected to the board of directors of the new United Fund. Following this was a motion to close nominations, which passed unanimously, so the whole slate was declared the duly elected board.

This was followed by a call for questions from the floor. I got up and, feeling I should somehow identify myself, began by saying that I represented a study group of stay-at-home mothers, all with preschool children. "We're a small group, but we all need to have something to think about when the kids are asleep and we're doing the dishes. So we've been looking at our community services—particularly those relating to family and child welfare. We meet once a month, on our one night out, to talk about what we've learned. We thought the proposed United Fund could work out to be the best plan for supporting our community services. We don't have a lot of money to give away," I continued, "so we'd like to be sure that whatever we're able to contribute will be well spent. We'd like a qualified expert from outside the city to do an evaluation of services currently offered, and to recommend the necessary standards to be required for admission to membership in the new Fund."

This elicited great applause. A woman immediately stood up and nominated me to the newly elected Board, despite that nominations were closed and the board already elected. (Another round of applause.) The chair, completely flummoxed, announced he'd accept the nomination. He didn't ask me if I accepted the nomination, nor did he call for a vote. No one protested this lapse in procedure, so, somewhat disconcerted, I became the only woman on the founding board of the Edmonton United Community Fund.

I wondered what I'd gotten into. I knew nothing about United Funds. So I wrote for advice from a friend at the University of Toronto School of Social Work. While waiting to hear back, I was called to the first meeting of the new Board. The chair, who was the CEO of the local gas company, announced at the top of the meeting that I had been appointed honorary treasurer. Since they didn't ask whether I would agree to the appointment, I took this to mean I wouldn't have to keep the books but would serve as an officer on the Executive and the Board. The chair then said that the first order of business was to sign the incorporation papers, which had already been prepared and were in the head office of his company. We were all to meet in that office the following week and sign the document.

When I got home, I found a letter from a friend telling me that a man named Larry Slade, who'd done his doctoral thesis on United Ways, had recently moved to Edmonton and would be glad to help. I phoned Larry and told him that although I knew nothing about United Funds, I had been elected to the Board of Directors and been asked to sign the incorporation papers, a document I hadn't seen. What should I look for?

"Just be sure it's not too thick," he said. "Incorporation papers usually contain only a rudimentary constitution. Bylaws come later, after a lot of study and discussion. The document shouldn't be much more than a couple of pages, just enough to get an organization started."

When I got to the office of the gas company late one afternoon the next week, the clerk pulled out a document about an inch and a half thick and pointed to the place I was to sign. I said, "I'd better read it first."

The clerk said, "I don't think it matters. Nobody else read it. They all just signed it. I'm just about ready to close the office and go home."

"Sorry, but I can't sign it without reading it. It's quite long. It will take me a bit of time."

She looked irritated at this, so I asked her if I could take it home. "Well, I'm in a hurry. I'm meeting a friend for dinner, so you better take it."

When I got home I called Larry, who agreed to meet me a couple of days later and go over the whole document. In the meantime the Board secretary phoned and said it was urgent that I sign the document as soon as possible. I said I was still going through it and would be in touch.

Larry and I spent some hours reading it and making notes. We found several problems. There was no minimum number for a quorum, no schedule for regular meetings, and the chair could call a meeting on three days' notice, a time-honoured way of making sure the "right" people were available for a crucial vote. There was also a curious provision that the Red Cross would be entitled to 15 percent of the total amount raised each year, regardless of other community requests or needs. While Jim was trying to round up someone from the congregation to type up our notes, I got an urgent phone call from the Board chair: "Mrs. Norquay, can you tell me when you'll be downtown with the signed papers? We need your name on that document as soon as possible."

"I've just finished carefully reading it, and I'm now making some notes. I'll get back to you very soon."

When our typist arrived, she said it would take at least a full day to do the typing and reference the notes to the relevant places in the document. The Board chair phoned again, trying to sound only slightly exasperated, and asked when I was going to sign. "We'd like it all done before our meeting next week."

"I don't think I can get downtown before the next meeting," I said. "I have a babysitter only once a week. But I'd like to talk to the whole Board before I sign anything. However, I certainly will come to the meeting."

"For God's sake, be sure you bring the papers. They never should have gone out of my office. Everyone's signature is there but yours. So be sure to come to the meeting, and bring the document."

On hanging up the phone, I began to feel a bit scared at what I'd taken on. Larry backed me up. "Just go and be a woman," he said. "Be worried, a bit scared, slightly fragile. Then they'll feel sorry for you and some will want to protect you. But while you're at it, make sure they read the whole thing—you've got our notes and you can point out the problems as you go through."

Having never thought of myself as fragile—but apprehensive nonetheless—I decided to dress as far up to the nines as my wardrobe would allow. I wore my most feminine dress and an elegant, floppy wide-brimmed hat my mother had bought for a wedding and passed on to me—a hat I'd never have worn under any other circumstances. I thought, thus dressed, I would look as if I had just come from the posh afternoon tea providentially being given by the University Women's Club that same day. And I hoped the summer I'd spent taking acting courses when I was nineteen would stand me in good stead.

When the meeting began, the chair informed us that it was important to get the incorporation papers signed so that we could get on with the organization. He had a heavy agenda and wanted to get the matter over and done with. "So, Mrs. Norquay, what was it that you wanted to talk about?"

"I've put several hours into studying the document and there are some serious issues that need discussion."

"For God's sake, let's get down to specifics."

"I've brought my notes, and I'll deal with the problems one at a time."

From a director: "Let's go! Let's go!"

"I'll try to be brief, but I've developed a rather bad headache and that may make things a bit difficult for me. I'll do the best I can. I'm not used to being the only woman."

Again from the chair: "Okay, okay! Let's hear it."

A caution from the secretary: "Come on, guys, don't push her, let her take her time." (Larry was right.)

I slowly pulled my notes out of my briefcase and began to read my carefully prepared introductory speech. "I discussed this document with a person whose professional expertise and intellectual capacities I greatly respect. He said that the kind of constitution this document provides for would inhibit free discussion, place power in the hands of a small group, and relieve the Board of any real responsibility. On examination, the incorporation papers appear to be a slightly warmed-over copy of the constitution and bylaws of the Community Chest, the organization you aspire to replace. There are a few changes. One of these is a clause guaranteeing the Red Cross a straight 15 percent of all the money raised in the annual campaign."

This was greeted with shock and total chaos:

"What?"

"I didn't know that."

"Nor did I."

"I can't believe it."

"That'll never fly."

"Who put that in?"

"That wasn't in the Community Chest constitution, so who put that in?"

"If that stays, the whole thing will fall apart."

Having been given this revelation, they decided to throw out the whole document and prepare a new set of papers with just the required minimum of clauses. *That* I agreed to sign.

Never before having been appointed honorary anything, I didn't find out until much later that honorary officers are not expected to be participating board members; they simply lend their name to the cause. So when they appointed me honorary treasurer, I guess they expected me just to sign the incorporation papers and glory in the honour of the title. But I didn't get the message. And I never found out who purloined the constitution of the Community Chest to use for the incorporation papers of the "new" United Community Fund, or who inserted the bylaw about the Red Cross.

twenty-three

Learning to Be a Woman

In the spring of 1960, when we were living in Edmonton, Jim decided to use his study leave to attend a sensitivity training workshop at the United Church Training Centre in the Qu'Appelle Valley in Saskatchewan. He proposed that I should enrol for the same training. I readily agreed. I hadn't been away from our children for more than a day since the birth of our youngest, and I was ready for a change. Sensitivity training was an educational invention in vogue at the time, designed to train people to work effectively with groups. Before embarking on what my mother called "taking holy orders," I'd had a career working with a variety of community groups and was intrigued with the idea of learning something new. Jim thought we could afford the trip, so we both planned to go. We had a greatly loved babysitter who agreed to live in for a week and a good friend in the congregation who would drop by and make sure all was well.

I looked forward to shedding my role as a minister's wife. I would simply be a participant, an equal among equals. I wouldn't have to worry about keeping out of trouble—something I seemed to have no difficulty getting into in a church setting. Jim was looking forward to some respite from pastoral concerns, and was leaving his clerical garb and persona at home. We got out our camp clothes, packed a few books in case there'd be time to read, and off we went.

Along with the other participants, we arrived at the centre in time for supper. The first evening was spent mainly in socializing, the stock phrase being "getting to know each other." To my dismay, the group consisted almost entirely of ministers, all men. There were only three women, myself and two deaconesses, probably in their fifties. It was not the heterogeneous mix of professionals I had expected and hoped for. However Brian Jones, someone we knew well, was there, and I was pleased about that. Brian had been the minister in Sangudo, the pastoral charge nearest to us, while we lived in Mayerthorpe. In those years, we were starved for any kind of serious discussion outside of church concerns. Brian and his wife used to drive fifteen miles over a meagrely gravelled highway a couple of times a year to have dinner with us. Into the wee hours we'd toss around ideas for the sheer fun of it: philosophy, politics, theology, novels we were reading—it didn't matter. Those evenings were lifesavers for all of us. So if Brian was here, it couldn't be too bad.

The workshop comprised lectures and exercises to practise the skills we were supposed to learn as well as meetings of the training group—the most crucial part of the program, we were told. The training group met every morning from nine until noon. Jim and I were told that ordinarily a husband and wife would not be allowed in the same training group, but the workshop didn't have enough registrants to create two groups, so we would have to work together. However, we were not to act as if we were married and were told that under no circumstances were we to jump to each other's defence in the heat of a training group discussion. Wondering what we'd need to be defended from, we looked forward to the morning as a unique experience.

The training group took place around an oval table, where all twelve of us, together with our two male facilitators, could see and hear one another. The first session began with one of the facilitators making a single opening remark, saying that the main order of business was to talk about what was going on in the group. Since nothing had yet gone on, we expected further instruction. But not a word was added to this announcement. The room fell silent. Finally someone said, "Don't you even have an agenda?"

No answer from the facilitators. Again, silence in the group. The discomfort was palpable, and finally someone burst out, "Let's make our own agenda." Immediately we were launched, arguing about what to talk about. Many of the early suggestions had to do with church problems, but the discussion branched out widely after that, with no attempt to find consensus. We moved aimlessly from topic to topic and became deeply involved only when something controversial emerged.

On the second morning, Jim was sounding off about something when Harold, the man sitting across from me, got quite agitated, pounded the table, and said, "That's a lie."

Having taken seriously the advice we were given not to defend each other, I asked, "Do you think he is deliberately lying or that he really believes what he is saying?"

Harold gave the table another bang and shouted, "Both."

Prepared to go on playing the game, I asked, "Do you think anyone else here behaves that way?"

Another hard bang, "Yes, you! You never mean what you say. You just put it all on. I don't like the way you talk. I don't like the way you look. I just don't like the way you behave."

Thinking I might learn something useful about myself, I said, "Is there anyone else here who feels that way about me?" And to my deep humiliation, several of the men around that table said yes. The two deaconesses remained silent, but most of the men joined in. They felt the same as Harold. I made them feel uncomfortable. They didn't like the way I talked. They didn't like my clothes. They didn't like women wearing pants. All of this came as a shock, because I'd rather enjoyed talking with several of them during that first social evening. Had they disliked me even then? Still hoping I might learn something, and willing to go on playing the game, I said I knew that sometimes I annoyed people, but I didn't know why. One of the reasons I'd come to the workshop was that I thought I might find out. Could anyone tell me? This was met by absolute silence. By this time, I was totally frustrated and angry. About to burst into tears, I left.

I went to the garden, my blood boiling, adrenalin rushing. I felt I needed to pound something. So I asked the groundskeeper whether there was anything that needed digging. He said all the shrubs needed to have the soil loosened, gave me a fork, and I started to work. In about half an hour the group came out. Brian came along right away to talk to me.

"Gosh, Marg," he said, "you really took a beating. You took much more than any of the rest of us would have."

I said I supposed so, and went on digging.

He went on: "I've been wondering, though. Don't you think you've always wished you were a man?"

I was stunned. I thought Brian was a friend. All I could say was I'd never thought of such a thing. Maybe it was there, deep in my subconscious, but, if so, it wasn't something I was aware of.

But Brian's question finally did me in. I knew I had to remove myself from the group until I could stabilize. So I walked back to our room with Jim and told him I wasn't going to dinner and I wasn't going back to the group. He said he understood—we'd both played by the rules—but the facilitators had let things go too far. He'd bring me my meals on a tray. I stayed incommunicado for a couple of days, reading the books we'd brought and trying to figure out what had happened.

The two facilitators finally came to see me on the second day of my absence. They wanted to know how I was feeling. I told them I was fine but completely frustrated. "What did I do that got everyone so mad at me? Did I put people down?"

They didn't think so.

"Didn't I listen to what others said?"

"Oh yes, you obviously listened because you always responded."

"Did I interrupt and not let others have their say?"

They said they didn't remember my doing that.

"Did I talk too much? What did I do?"

They had no answer. But when I persisted and said there must be something, they finally said, with some hesitation, "Well, you do have a lot of ideas—but don't worry about it." And with that they left.

But I now had considerable food for thought. Maybe I didn't quite fit their idea of what a woman should be or, heaven help me, what a minister's wife should be. The two deaconesses had remained silent most of the time, taking no part in any serious discussion. One of them had knitted throughout the sessions at which I had been present. The next morning was the last day, and I wasn't going to just ignominiously disappear. What to do?

Jim told me that after I left the group, the private discussions between sessions and in the evenings had focused on what to do about Harold. They thought he was in need of help. How could they see that he got some kind of counselling when he got back to his parish? A clear case of the blind leading the blind, I thought. They apparently didn't think *I* needed help. But with this news, my equilibrium was restored.

I went to see Aggie, the dean of the Training Centre. I didn't tell her what had happened but asked if she had some large knitting needles and some thick balls of wool. She did and, without asking any questions, got them out and gave them to me. After eating my supper once more on a tray, I spent the last evening knitting a long red scarf about a foot wide. I hadn't known ministers' wives were not supposed to wear slacks, but in case the weather might become too warm for woollen slacks and sweaters, I took the precaution of packing a light cotton summer dress. It was a rather feminine creation, with a flared skirt and floppy short sleeves. The weather hadn't warmed, but I decided to wear the dress the next morning anyway. There was sure to be enough heat in the training group to warm me up if I needed it. I took my place, with my wool and knitting needles, the scarf now down to my knees, and sat through the whole three hours without saying a word. I just knitted. When the session was over, everyone rushed to check out on time. But I remained seated, pulled out the needles, started to unravel the scarf, which now reached the floor, and rolled the wool back into a ball. No one noticed or said goodbye.

While reflecting on this story, I realize that the men genuinely didn't know why they were upset with me. When I pressed them to tell me what I did to annoy them, they were silent. Brian's way of understanding the situation was to assume I must always have wanted to be a man, but he didn't tell me why he thought this. There weren't words yet to explain the discomfort or fear some men feel if a women dares to think of herself as an equal in a group where all other equals are men.

This experience is my most vivid memory of being expected to conform to men's notions of the woman they wanted me to be. But it is not a story of failure, it's one of beginning. Eventually I learned to express my point of view in a gentler way than I might otherwise have done.

In the years that followed, I raised my family, had a career, and collaborated with other women who, like me, wanted to contribute to their community. And now multitudes of women are striving to be themselves and learning to be women in their own particular way while we cheer each other on.

LIFE WRITING SERIES

In the **Life Writing Series**, Wilfrid Laurier University Press publishes life writing and new life-writing criticism and theory in order to promote autobiographical accounts, diaries, letters, and testimonials written and/or told by women and men whose political, literary, or philosophical purposes are central to their lives. The Series features accounts written in English, or translated into English from French or the languages of the First Nations, or any of the languages of immigration to Canada.

From its inception, **Life Writing** has aimed to foreground the stories of those who may never have imagined themselves as writers or as people with lives worthy of being (re)told. Its readership has expanded to include scholars, youth, and avid general readers both in Canada and abroad. The Series hopes to continue its work as a leading publisher of life writing of all kinds, as an imprint that aims for both broad representation and scholarly excellence, and as a tool for both historical and autobiographical research.

As its mandate stipulates, the Series privileges those individuals and communities whose stories may not, under normal circumstances, find a welcoming home with a publisher. **Life Writing** also publishes original theoretical investigations about life writing, as long as they are not limited to one author or text.

Series Editor
Marlene Kadar
Humanities Division, York University

Manuscripts to be sent to
Lisa Quinn, Acquisitions Editor
Wilfrid Laurier University Press
75 University Avenue West
Waterloo, Ontario, Canada N2L 3C5

Books in the Life Writing Series
Published by Wilfrid Laurier University Press

Haven't Any News: Ruby's Letters from the Fifties edited by Edna Staebler with an Afterword by Marlene Kadar • 1995 / x + 165 pp. / ISBN 0-88920-248-6

"I Want to Join Your Club": Letters from Rural Children, 1900–1920 edited by Norah L. Lewis with a Preface by Neil Sutherland • 1996 / xii + 250 pp. (30 b & w photos) / ISBN 0-88920-260-5

And Peace Never Came by Elisabeth M. Raab with Historical Notes by Marlene Kadar • 1996 / x + 196 pp. (12 b & w photos, map) / ISBN 0-88920-281-8

Dear Editor and Friends: Letters from Rural Women of the North-West, 1900–1920 edited by Norah L. Lewis • 1998 / xvi + 166 pp. (20 b & w photos) / ISBN 0-88920-287-7

The Surprise of My Life: An Autobiography by Claire Drainie Taylor with a Foreword by Marlene Kadar • 1998 / xii + 268 pp. (8 colour photos and 92 b & w photos) / ISBN 0-88920-302-4

Memoirs from Away: A New Found Land Girlhood by Helen M. Buss / Margaret Clarke • 1998 / xvi + 153 pp. / ISBN 0-88920-350-4

The Life and Letters of Annie Leake Tuttle: Working for the Best by Marilyn Färdig Whiteley • 1999 / xviii + 150 pp. / ISBN 0-88920-330-x

Marian Engel's Notebooks: "Ah, mon cahier, écoute" edited by Christl Verduyn • 1999 / viii + 576 pp. / ISBN 0-88920-333-4 cloth / ISBN 0-88920-349-0 paper

Be Good Sweet Maid: The Trials of Dorothy Joudrie by Audrey Andrews • 1999 / vi + 276 pp. / ISBN 0-88920-334-2

Working in Women's Archives: Researching Women's Private Literature and Archival Documents edited by Helen M. Buss and Marlene Kadar • 2001 / vi + 120 pp. / ISBN 0-88920-341-5

Repossessing the World: Reading Memoirs by Contemporary Women by Helen M. Buss • 2002 / xxvi + 206 pp. / ISBN 0-88920-408-x cloth / ISBN 0-88920-410-1 paper

Chasing the Comet: A Scottish-Canadian Life by Patricia Koretchuk • 2002 / xx + 244 pp. / ISBN 0-88920-407-1

The Queen of Peace Room by Magie Dominic • 2002 / xii + 115 pp. / ISBN 0-88920-417-9

China Diary: The Life of Mary Austin Endicott by Shirley Jane Endicott • 2002 / xvi + 251 pp. / ISBN 0-88920-412-8

The Curtain: Witness and Memory in Wartime Holland by Henry G. Schogt • 2003 / xii + 132 pp. / ISBN 0-88920-396-2

Teaching Places by Audrey J. Whitson • 2003 / xiii + 178 pp. / ISBN 0-88920-425-X

Through the Hitler Line by Laurence F. Wilmot, M.C. • 2003 / xvi + 152 pp. / ISBN 0-88920-448-9

Where I Come From by Vijay Agnew • 2003 / xiv + 298 pp. / ISBN 0-88920-414-4

The Water Lily Pond by Han Z. Li • 2004 / x + 254 pp. / ISBN 0-88920-431-4

The Life Writings of Mary Baker McQuesten: Victorian Matriarch edited by Mary J. Anderson • 2004 / xxii + 338 pp. / ISBN 0-88920-437-3

Seven Eggs Today: The Diaries of Mary Armstrong, 1859 and 1869 edited by Jackson W. Armstrong • 2004 / xvi + 228 pp. / ISBN 0-88920-440-3

Love and War in London: A Woman's Diary 1939–1942 by Olivia Cockett; edited by Robert W. Malcolmson • 2005 / xvi + 208 pp. / ISBN 0-88920-458-6

Incorrigible by Velma Demerson • 2004 / vi + 178 pp. / ISBN 0-88920-444-6

Auto/biography in Canada: Critical Directions edited by Julie Rak • 2005 / viii + 264 pp. / ISBN 0-88920-478-0

Tracing the Autobiographical edited by Marlene Kadar, Linda Warley, Jeanne Perreault, and Susanna Egan • 2005 / viii + 280 pp. / ISBN 0-88920-476-4

Must Write: Edna Staebler's Diaries edited by Christl Verduyn • 2005 / viii + 304 pp. / ISBN 0-88920-481-0

Food That Really Schmecks by Edna Staebler • 2007 / xxiv + 334 pp. / ISBN 978-0-88920-521-5

163256: A Memoir of Resistance by Michael Englishman • 2007 / xvi + 112 pp. (14 b&w photos) / ISBN 978-1-55458-009-5

The Wartime Letters of Leslie and Cecil Frost, 1915–1919 edited by R.B. Fleming • 2007 / xxxvi + 384 pp. (49 b&w photos, 5 maps) / ISBN 978-1-55458-000-2

Johanna Krause Twice Persecuted: Surviving in Nazi Germany and Communist East Germany by Carolyn Gammon and Christiane Hemker • 2007 / x + 170 pp. (58 b&w photos, 2 maps) / ISBN 978-1-55458-006-4

Watermelon Syrup: A Novel by Annie Jacobsen with Jane Finlay-Young and Di Brandt • 2007 / x + 268 pp. / ISBN 978-1-55458-005-7

Becoming My Mother's Daughter: A Story of Survival and Renewal by Erika Gottlieb • 2008 / x + 178 pp. (36 b&w illus., 17 colour) / ISBN 978-1-55458-030-9

Broad Is the Way: Stories from Mayerthorpe by Margaret Norquay • 2008 / x + 106 pp. (6 b&w photos) / ISBN 978-1-55458-020-0